IN PRAISE
OF CHURCHES

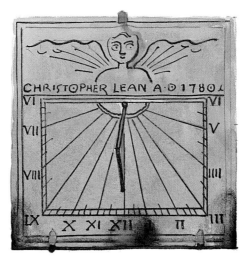

Long Compton
Parish Church
Warwickshire

John Betjeman

In Praise
of Churches

With
Paul Hogarth

John Murray
Albemarle Street, London

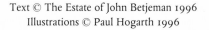

A catalogue record for this book is available from
the British Library

ISBN 0–7195–5554–X

Colour Separations – Dot Gradations
Typeset in 12pt Columbus by Wearset, Boldon, Tyne and Wear.
Printed and bound in Great Britain by Butler & Tanner Limited,
Frome and London.

Contents

CHURCH CRAWLING

I KNOW NO GREATER PLEASURE than church-crawling. It leads you to the remotest and quietest country. It introduces you to the history of England in stone and wood and glass which is always truer than what you read in books. You meet all sorts of people on your travels.

It was through looking at churches that I came to believe in the reason why, despite neglect and contempt, innovation and business bishops, they still survive and continue to grow and prosper, especially in our industrial towns.

You must have the instruments of a church-crawler. The first of these is a map. A one-inch ordnance map (no others will do) tells you whether the church has a tower or spire for it is marked with a cross and a black square if it is a tower, a cross or a black circle if it is a spire. You can generally assume that a country church is old, even if it has no tower or spire, if the map shows dotted lines of footpaths leading to it.

The next thing you need is an eye. Look at the church for what it is, a place of worship and a piece of architecture combined. Guide books will tell you that something is in the 'debased' style, meaning that it was built in the sixteenth, seventeenth or eighteenth centuries, but it does not matter when it was built or whether it is 'pure' or 'debased'. What does matter is, do you like the look of it yourself?

Instead of bothering about dates and what the guide books say, use your eyes.

THE OLD CHURCHES

THE PARISH CHURCHES OF ENGLAND are even more varied than the landscape. The tall town church, smelling of furniture polish and hot-water pipes, a shadow of the medieval marvel it once was, so assiduously have Victorian restorers renewed everything old; the little weather-beaten church standing in a farmyard down a narrow lane, bat-droppings over the pews and one service a month; the relic of the 15th-century wool trade, whose soaring splendour of stone and glass subsequent generations have had neither the energy nor the money to destroy; the suburban church with Northamptonshire steeple calling with mid-Victorian bells to the ghosts of merchant carriage folk; the tin chapel-of-ease on the industrial estate; the High and the Low churches, the alive and the dead ones, the churches that are easy to pray in and those that are not, the churches whose architecture brings you to your knees, the churches whose decorations affront the sight – all these come within the wide Anglican embrace.

Chipping Campden Church of St James & Almshouses

From the first wooden church put up in a forest clearing or stone cell on windy moor to the newest social hall, with sanctuary and altar partitioned off, our churches have existed chiefly for the celebration of what some call the Mass, or the Eucharist, and others call Holy Communion or the Lord's Supper. Between the early paganism of Britain and the present paganism there are nearly twenty thousand churches and well over a thousand years of Christianity. More than half the buildings are medieval, but many have been so severely restored that they could almost be called Victorian. If there is anything old about them it is what one can discern through the detective work of the visual imagination.

THE CHURCHYARD

Tombs & Topiary, St Mary, Painswick/Glos

SEE ON SOME VILLAGE MOUND, in the mind's eye, the parish church of today. It is in the old part of the place. Near the church will be the few old houses of the parish, and almost for certain there will be an inn very near the church. A lych-gate built as a memorial at the beginning of this century indicates the entrance to the churchyard. Away on the outskirts of the town or village, if it is a place of any size, will be the arid new cemetery consecrated in 1910 when there was no more room in the churchyard.

Nearer to the church and almost always on the south side are to be found the older tombs, the examples of fine craftsmanship in local stone of the Queen Anne and Georgian periods. Wool merchants and big farmers, all those not entitled to an armorial monument on the walls inside the church, generally occupy the grandest graves. Their obelisks, urns and table tombs are surrounded with Georgian iron-work. Parish clerks, smaller farmers and tradesmen lie below plainer stones. All their families are recorded in deep-cut lettering. Here is a flourish of calligraphy; there is reproduced the typeface of Baskerville. The tradition lasted until the middle of the 19th century in those country places where stone was used as easily as wood. Some old craftsman was carving away while the young go-aheads in the nearest town were busy inserting machine-made letters into white Italian marble.

The elegance of the local stone carver's craft is not to be seen only in the lettering. In the 18th century it was the convention to carve symbols round the top of the headstone and down the sides. The earlier examples are in bold relief, cherubs with plough-boy faces and thick wings, and scythes, hour glasses and skulls and cross-bones diversify their tops. You will find in one or another country churchyard that there has been a local sculptor of unusual vigour and perhaps genius who has even carved a rural scene above some well-graven name. Towards the end of the 18th century the lettering becomes finer and more prominent, the decoration flatter and more conventional, usually in the Adam manner, as though a son had taken on his father's business and depended on architectural pattern-books. But the tops of all headstones varied in shape. At this time too it became the custom in some districts to paint the stones and to add a little gold leaf to the lettering. Paint and stone by now have acquired a varied pattern produced by weather and fungus, so that the stones are probably more beautiful than they were when they were new, splodged as they are with gold and silver and slightly over-grown with moss. On a sharp frosty day when the sun is in the south and throwing up the carving, or in the west and bringing out all the colour of the lichens, a country

churchyard may bring back the lost ages of craftsmanship more effectively than the church which stands behind it. Those unknown carvers belong to the world of wheelwrights and wagon-makers. They are of the same race as produced the vigorous inn signs which were such a feature of England before the brewers ruined them with artiness and standardisation.

From Churchyards

Now when the weather starts to clear
How fresh the primrose clumps appear,
Those shining pools of springtime flower
In our churchyard. And on the tower
We see the sharp spring sunlight thrown
On all its sparkling rainwashed stone,
That tower, so built to take the light
Of sun by day and moon by night,
That centuries of weather there
Have mellowed it to twice as fair
As when it first rose new and hard
Above the sports in our churchyard.
   For churchyards then, though hallowed ground
Were not so grim as now they sound,
And horns of ale were handed round
For which churchwardens used to pay

On each especial vestry day.
'Twas thus the village drunk its beer
With its relations buried near,
And that is why we often see
Inns where the alehouse used to be
Close to the church when prayers were said
And Masses for the village dead.
　　Our churches are our history shown
In wood and glass and iron and stone.
I hate to see in old churchyards
Tombstones stacked round like playing cards
Along the wall which then encloses
A trim new lawn and standard roses,
Bird-baths and objects such as fill a
Garden in some suburban villa.
The Bishop comes; the bird-bath's blessed,
Our churchyard's now 'a garden of rest'.
And so it may be, all the same
Graveyard's a much more honest name.
　　Oh why do people waste their breath
Inventing dainty names for death?
On the old tombstones of the past
We do not read 'At peace at last'
But simply 'died' or plain 'departed'.
It's no good being chicken-hearted.
We die; that's that; our flesh decays
Or disappears in other ways.
But since we're Christians, we believe
That we new bodies will receive
To clothe our souls for us to meet
Our Maker at his Judgement Seat.

THE OUTSIDE OF THE CHURCH

THE CHURCH WHOSE SOUTHERN side we are approaching is probably little like the building which stood there even two centuries before, although it has not been rebuilt. The outside walls were probably plastered. Churches which are ashlar-faced all over are rare, but many have an ashlar-faced western tower, or aisle to the north-east or south-east, or a porch or transept built of cut stone in the 15th century by a rich family. Plaster made of a mixture of hair or straw and sand and lime was from Saxon times applied as a covering to the walls. Only the cut stone round the windows and doors was left, and even this was lime-washed. The plaster was thin and uneven. It was beautifully coloured a pale yellow or pink or white according to the tradition of the district. And if it has now been stripped off the church, it may still be seen on old cottages of the village if any survive.

And this is the place to say that most of the old parish churches in England are building rather than architecture. They are gradual growths, as their outside walls will show; in their construction they partake of the character of cottages and barns and the early manor house, and not of the great abbey churches built for monks or secular canons. Their humble builders were inspired to copy what was to be seen in the nearest great church. The styles of Gothic came from these large buildings, but the village execution of them was later and could rarely rise to more than window tracery and roof timbering. Even these effects have a local flavour, they are a village voluntary compared with the music played on a great instrument by the cathedral organist. Of course here and there, when the abbeys declined, a famous mason from an abbey or cathedral might rebuild the church of his native place, and masons were employed in rich wool districts of East Anglia, the Midlands and parts of Yorkshire and Devon to build large churches which really are architecture and the product of a single brain, not the humble expression of a village community's worship.

Old paintings sometimes show the external roofs as they used to be. The church roof and chancel are scarcely distinguishable from the cottage roofs. If the original steep pitch survives, it is seen to be covered with the local tiles, stones or thatch of the old houses of the district. Fifteenth-century and Georgian raisings or lowerings of the roof and alterations to a flatter pitch generally meant a re-covering with lead,

and the original pitch may be traced on the eastern face of the tower. Victorian restorers much enjoyed raising roofs to what they considered the original pitch, or putting on an altogether new roof in the cathedral manner. The effect of those re-roofings is generally the most obviously new feature on the outside of an old church. Red tiles and patterned slates from Wales or stone tiles which continually come down because they are set at a pitch too steep for their weight, are the usual materials. Instead of being graded in size, large at the eaves and getting smaller as they reach the ridge, the stone tiles are all of the same size so that the roof is not proportioned to the walls. The ridges are usually crowned with ridge tiles of an ornamental pattern which contrast in colour and texture with the rest. The gable ends are adorned with crosses. The drainage system is prominent and there will be pipes running down the wall to a gutter. On the rain-water heads at the top of these pipes there will probably be the date of the restoration. The old way of draining a roof was generally by leaden or wooden spouts rushing out of the mouths of gargoyles and carrying the water well beyond the walls of the church into the churchyard. Gargoyles can be fearsome, particularly on the north side of the church, and heads and statues, where they have survived Puritan outrage and Victorian zeal, are sometimes extremely beautiful or fantastic.

The church porch flapping with electoral rolls, notices of local acts, missionary appeals and church services gives us a welcome. Most church porches in England are built on the south side, first as a protection for the door from prevailing south-west gales. Then they were used as places for baptism, bargains were made there, oaths sworn, and burial and marriage services conducted. Above some of them, from the 14th century onwards, a room was built, usually for keeping parish chests and records. In these places many a village school was started. At first they may have been inhabited by a watchman, who could look down into the church from an internal window.

Notice the stonework round the outside doors. Often it is roundheaded and of Norman date, an elaborate affair of several concentric semi-circles of carved stone. It may even be the only Norman work left in the church and may originally have been the chancel arch before the chancel was enlarged and a screen put across its western end. The later medieval rebuilders respected the Norman craftsmanship and often kept a Norman door inside their elaborate porches.

There is often difficulty in opening the door. This gives the less impatient of us a chance of looking at the door itself. Either because the business of transferring the huge church lock was too difficult, or because here was a good piece of wood older than any of the trees in the parish, church doors have survived from the middle ages while the interiors on to which they open have been repaired out of recognition. The wood of the door may be carved or be decorated with old local ironwork. If it is an old door it will invariably open inwards. So first turn the iron handle and push hard. Then if the door seems to be locked, turn the handle the other way and push hard. Then feel on the wall-plate of the porch for the key. Then look under the mat. Then lift the notice-board from the porch wall and look behind that. Then look inside the lamp bracket outside the porch. Church keys are usually six or eight inches long and easy to find. If there is no sign of the key and all vestry doors are locked, call at a house. If the path leading through the churchyard to a door in the vicarage wall is overgrown and looks unused, you may be sure the vicarage has been sold to wealthy unbelievers and there is no chance of getting the key from there. The houses to choose are those with pots of flowers in the window. Here will be living traditional villagers who even if they are chapel will probably know who it is who keeps the church key. Men are less likely to know than women, since men in villages are more rarely churchgoers. Villagers are all out on Saturday afternoons shopping in the local town. Only an idiot and the dog remain behind.

Norman doorway with Ram's head moulding, St Peter's Windrush, Glos

THE BELLS

BELL RINGING IN ENGLAND is known among ringers as 'the exercise', rather as the rearing and training of pigeons is known among the pigeon fraternity as 'the fancy'. It is a class-less folk art which has survived in the church despite all arguments about doctrine and the diminution of congregations. In many a church when the parson opens with the words 'Dearly beloved brethren, the Scripture moveth us in sundry places . . .' one may hear the tramp of the ringers descending the newel stair into the refreshing silence of the graveyard. Though in some churches they may come in later by the main door and sit in the pew marked 'Ringers Only', in others they will not be seen again, the sweet melancholy notes of 'the exercise' floating out over the Sunday chimney-pots having been their contribution to the glory of God.

A belfry where ringers are keen has the used and admired look of a social club. There, above the little bit of looking-glass in which the ringers slick their hair and straighten their ties before stepping down into the outside world, you will find blackboards with gilded lettering proclaiming past peals rung for hours at a stretch. In another place will be the rules of the tower written in a clerkly hand. A charming Georgian ringers' rhyme survives at St. Endellion, Cornwall, on a board headed with a picture of ringers in knee-breeches:

> *We ring the Quick to Church and dead to Grave,*
>
> *Good is our use, such usage let us have*
>
> *Who here therefore doth Damn, or Curse or Swear,*
>
> *Or strike in Quarrel thogh no Blood appear,*
>
> *Who wears a Hatt or Spurr or turns a Bell*
>
> *Or by unskilful handling spoils a Peal,*
>
> *Shall Sixpence pay for every single Crime*
>
> *'Twill make him careful 'gainst another time.*
>
> *Let all in Love and Friendship hither come,*
>
> *Whilst the shrill Treble calls to Thundering Tom,*
>
> *And since bells are our modest Recreation*
>
> *Let's Rise and Ring and Fall to Admiration.*

Many country towers have six bells. Not all these bells are medieval. Most were cast in the 17th, 18th or 19th centuries when change-ringing was becoming a country exercise. And the older bells will have been re-cast during that time, to bring them into tune with the new ones. They are likely to have been again re-cast in modern times, and the ancient inscription preserved and welded on to the re-cast bell.

The older bells have beautiful lettering sometimes, as at Somerby and South Somercotes in Lincolnshire, where they are inscribed with initial letters decorated with figures so that they look like illuminated initials from old manuscripts interpreted in relief on metal. The English love for Our Lady survived in inscriptions on church bells long after the Reformation, as did the use of Latin. Many 18th and even early 19th-century bells have Latin inscriptions. A rich collection of varied dates may be seen by struggling about on the wooden cage in which the bells hang among the bat-droppings in the tower.

Pub Sign, TAUNTON, Somerset

Bristol

Green upon the flooded Avon shone the after-storm-wet-sky
Quick the struggling withy branches let the leaves of autumn fly
And a star shone over Bristol, wonderfully far and high.

Ringers in an oil-lit belfry – Bitton? Kelston? who shall say –
Smoothly practising a plain course, caverned out the dying day
As their melancholy music flooded up and ebbed away.

Then all Somerset was round me and I saw the clippers ride,
High above the moonlit houses, triple-masted on the tide,
By the tall embattled church-towers of the Bristol waterside.

And an undersong to branches dripping into pools and wells
Out of multitudes of elm trees over leagues of hills and dells
Was the mathematic pattern of a plain course on the bells.

Bristol skyline

THE INTERIOR TODAY

As we sit in a back pew of the nave with the rest of the congregation – the front pews are reserved for those who never come to church – most objects which catch the eye are Victorian. What we see of the present age is cheap and sparse. The thick wires clamped on to the old outside wall, which make the church look as though the Vicar had put it on the telephone, are an indication without that electric light has lately been introduced. The position of the lights destroys the effect of the old mouldings on arches and columns. It is a light too harsh and bright for an old building, and the few remaining delicate textures on stone and walls are destroyed by the dazzling floodlights fixed in reflectors from the roof, and a couple of spotlights behind the chancel arch which throw their full radiance on the brass altar vases and on the Vicar when he marches up to give the blessing. At sermon time, in a winter evensong, the lights are switched off, and the strip reading-lamp on the pulpit throws up the vicar's chin and eyebrows so that he looks like Grock. A further disfigurement introduced by electrical engineers is a collection of meters, pipes and fuses on one of the walls. If a church must be lit with electricity – which is in any case preferable to gas, which streaks the walls – the advice of Sir Ninian Comper might well be taken. This is to have as many bulbs as possible of as low power as possible, so that they do not dazzle the eye when they hang from the roof and walls. Candles are the perfect lighting for an old church, and oil light is also effective. The mystery of an old church, however small the building, is preserved by irregularly placed clusters of low-powered bulbs which light service books but leave the roof in comparative darkness. The chancel should not be strongly lit, for this makes the church look small, and all too rarely are chancel and altar worthy of a brilliant light. I have hardly ever seen an electrically lit church where this method has been employed, and we may assume that the one in which we are sitting is either floodlit or strung with blinding pendants whose bulbs are covered by 'temporary' shades reminiscent of a Government office.

Other modern adornments are best seen in daylight, and it is in daylight that we will imagine the rest of the church. The 'children's corner' in front of the side altar, with its pale reproductions of water-colours by Margaret W. Tarrant, the powder-blue hangings and unstained oak kneelers, the side altar itself, too small in relation to the aisle window above it, the pale stained-glass figure of St. George with plenty of clear glass round it (Diocesan Advisory Committees do not like exclusion of daylight) or the anaemic stained-glass soldier in khaki – these are likely to be the only recent additions to the church, excepting a few mural tablets in oak or Hopton Wood stone, much too small in comparison with the 18th century ones, dotted about on the walls and giving them the appearance of a stamp album; these, thank goodness, are the only damage our age will have felt empowered to do.

Uffington

Tonight we feel the muffled peal
  Hang on the village like a pall;
It overwhelms the towering elms –
  That death-reminding dying fall;
The very sky no longer high
  Comes down within the reach of all.
Imprisoned in a cage of sound
Even the trivial seems profound.

Note: At different times in his life Uffington and Wantage were Betjeman's local parish churches.

On Leaving Wantage 1972

I like the way these old brick garden walls
Unevenly run down to Letcombe Brook.
I like the mist of green about the elms
In earliest leaf-time. More intensely green
The duck-weed undulates; a mud-grey trout
Hovers and darts away at my approach.

From rumpled beds on far-off new estates,
From houses over shops along the square,
From red-brick villas somewhat further out,
Ringers arrive, converging on the tower.
Third Sunday after Easter. Public ways
Reek faintly yet of last night's fish and chips.
The plumes of smoke from upright chimney-pots
Denote the death of last week's Sunday press,
While this week's waits on many a step and sill
Unopened, folded, supplements and all.

Suddenly on the unsuspecting air
The bells clash out. It seems a miracle
That leaf and flower should never even stir
In such great waves of medieval sound:
They ripple over roofs to fields and farms
So that 'the fellowship of Christ's religion'
Is roused to breakfast, church or sleep again.

From this wide vale, where all our married lives
We two have lived, we now are whirled away
Momently clinging to the things we knew –
Friends, footpaths, hedges, house and animals –
Till, borne along like twigs and bits of straw,
We sink below the sliding stream of time.

Hymn

The Church's Restoration
  In eighteen-eighty-three
Has left for contemplation
  Not what there used to be.
How well the ancient woodwork
  Looks round the Rect'ry hall,
Memorial of the good work
  Of him who plann'd it all.

He who took down the pew-ends
  And sold them anywhere
But kindly spared a few ends
  Work'd up into a chair.
O worthy persecution
  Of dust! O hue divine!
O cheerful substitution,
  Thou varnishéd pitch-pine!

Church furnishing! Church furnishing!
  Sing art and crafty praise!
He gave the brass for burnishing
  He gave the thick red baize,
He gave the new addition,
  Pull'd down the dull old aisle,
– To pave the sweet transition
  He gave th' encaustic tile.

Of marble brown and veinéd
  He did the pulpit make;
He order'd windows stainéd

Light red and crimson lake.
Sing on, with hymns uproarious,
   Ye humble and aloof,
Look up! and oh how glorious
   He has restored the roof!

The Interior in 1860

I N THOSE RICHER DAYS when a British passport was respected
throughout the world, when 'carriage folk' existed and there
was a smell of straw and stable in town streets and bobbing
tenants at lodge gates in the country, when it was unusual to boast of
disbelief in God and when 'Chapel' was connected with 'trade' and
'Church' with 'gentry', when there were many people in villages who
had never seen a train nor left their parish, when old farm-workers
still wore smocks, when town slums were newer and even more horri-
ble, when people had orchids in their conservatories and geraniums
and lobelias in the trim beds beside their gravel walks, when stained
glass was brownish-green and when things that shone were considered beautiful, whether they were pink granite, brass, pitchpine,
mahogany or encaustic tiles, when the rector was second only to the
squire, when the servants went to church in the evening, when there
were family prayers and basement kitchens – in those days God
seemed to have created the universe and to have sent His Son to
redeem the world, and there was a church parade to worship Him on
those shining Sunday mornings we read of in Charlotte M. Yonge's
novels and feel in Trollope and see in the drawings in *Punch*. Then it
was that the money pouring in from our empire was spent in restoring
old churches and in building bold and handsome new ones in crowded areas and exclusive suburbs, in seaside towns and dockland settle-
ments.

The aisles are crowded and the prevailing colours of clothes are
black, dark blue and purple. The gentlemen are in frock coats and lean
forward into their top hats for a moment's prayer, while the lesser men
are in black broad-cloth and sit with folded arms awaiting the rector.
He comes in after his curate and they sit at desks facing each other on
either side of the chancel steps. Both wear surplices: the Rector's is
long and flowing and he has a black scarf round his shoulders: so has
the curate, but his surplice is shorter and he wears a cassock under-
neath, for, if the truth be told, the curate is 'higher' than the rector
and would have no objection to wearing a coloured stole and seeing
a couple of candles lit on the altar for Holy Communion. But this
would cause grave scandal to the parishioners, who fear idolatry. The
surpliced choir precede the clergy and march out of the new vestry

Victorian Gasolier   St Saviours, Tetbury Glos

built on the north-east corner of the church. Some of the older men, feeling a little ridiculous in surplices, look wistfully towards the west end where the gallery used to be and where they sang as youths to serpent, fiddle and bass recorder in the old-fashioned choir, before the pipe organ was introduced up there in the chancel. The altar has been raised on a series of steps, the shining new tiles becoming more elaborate and brilliant the nearer they approach the altar. The altar frontal has been embroidered by ladies in the parish, a pattern of lilies on a red background. There is still an alms dish on the altar, and behind it a cross has been set in stone on the east wall. In ten years' time brass vases of flowers, a cross and candlesticks will be on a 'gradine' or shelf above the altar. The east window is new, tracery and all. The glass is green and red, showing the Ascension – the Crucifixion is a little ritualistic – and has been done by a London firm. And a smart London architect designed all these choir stalls in oak and these pews of pitch-pine in the nave and aisles. At his orders the new chancel roof was constructed, the plaster was taken off the walls of the church, and the stone floors were taken up and transformed into a shining stretch of red and black tiles. He also had that pale pink and yellow glass put in all the unstained windows so that a religious light was cast. The brass gas brackets are by Skidmore of Coventry. Some antiquarian remains are carefully preserved. A Norman capital from the old aisle which was pulled down, a pillar piscina, a half of a cusped arch which might have been – no one knows quite *what* it might have been, but it is obviously ancient. Unfortunately it was not possible to remove the pagan classical memorials of the last century owing to trouble about faculties and fear of offending the descendants of the families commemorated. The church is as good as new, and all in the medieval style of the middle-pointed period – the best period because it is in the middle and not 'crude' like Norman and Early English, or 'debased' like Perpendicular and Tudor. Nearly everyone can see the altar. The Jacobean pulpit has survived, lowered and re-erected on a stone base. Marble pulpits are rather expensive, and Jacobean is not wholly unfashionable so far as woodwork is concerned. The prevailing colours of the church are brown and green, with faint tinges of pink and yellow.

The Church in Georgian Times

St Katherine, Chiselhampton, OXON

S EE NOW THE OUTSIDE of our church about eighty years before, in, let us say, 1805, when the two folio volumes on the county were produced by a learned antiquarian, with aquatint engravings of the churches, careful copper-plates of fonts and supposedly Roman pieces of stone, and laborious copyings of entries in parish rolls. How different from the polished, furbished fane we have just left is this humble, almost cottage-like place of worship. Oak posts and rails enclose the churchyard in which a horse, maybe the Reverend Dr. Syntax's mare Grizzel, is grazing. The stones are humble and few, and lean this way and that on the south side. They are painted black and grey and the lettering on some is picked out in gold. Two altar tombs, one with a sculptured urn above it, are enclosed in sturdy iron rails such as one sees above the basements of Georgian terrace houses. Beyond the church below a thunderous sky we see the elm and oak landscape of an England comparatively unenclosed. Thatched cottages and stone-tiled farms are collected round the church, and beyond them on the boundaries of the parish the land is still open and park-like, while an unfenced road winds on with its freight of huge bonnetted wagons.

Sympathetic descriptive accounts of unrestored churches are rarely found in late Georgian or early Victorian prose or verse. Most of the writers on churches are antiquarians who see nothing but ancient stones, or whose zeal for 'restoration' colours their writing. The entertaining *Church-Goer* of Bristol thus describes the Somerset church of Brean. 'On the other side of the way stood the church – little and old, and unpicturesquely freshened up with whitewash and yellow ochre; the former on the walls and the latter on the worn stone mullions of the small Gothic windows. The stunted slate-topped tower was whitelimed, too – all but a little slate slab on the western side, which bore the inscription: JOHN GHENKIN, Churchwarden, 1729. Anything owing less to taste and trouble than the little structure you would not imagine. Though rude, however, and old, and kept together as it was by repeated whitewashings, which mercifully filled up flaws and cracks, it was not disproportioned or unmemorable in aspect, and might with a trifling outlay be made to look as though someone cared for it.'

Such a church with tracery ochred on the outside may be seen in the background of Millais' painting *The Blind Girl*. It is, I believe, Winchelsea before restoration. It is still possible to find an unrestored church. Almost every county has one or two.

Inside, high pews crowd the church. The nave is a forest of woodwork. The pews have doors to them. The panelling inside the pews is lined with baize, blue in one pew, red in another, green in another, and the baize is attached to the wood by brass studs such as one may see on the velvet-covered coffins in family vaults. Some very big pews will have fire-places. When one sits down, only the pulpit is visible from the pew, and the tops of the arches of the nave whose stonework will be washed with ochre, while the walls will be white or pale pink, green or blue. A satire on this sort of seating was published by John Noake in 1851:

> O my own darling pue, which might serve for a bed,
>
> With its cushions so soft and its curtains of red;
>
> Of my half waking visions that pue is the theme,
>
> And when sleep seals my eyes, of my pue still I dream.
>
> Foul fall the despoiler, whose ruthless award
>
> Has condemned me to squat, like the poor, on a board,
>
> To be crowded and shov'd, as I sit at my prayers,
>
> As though my devotions could mingle with theirs.
>
> I have no vulgar pride, oh dear me, not I,
>
> But still I must say I could never see why
>
> We give them room to sit, to stand or to kneel,
>
> As if they, like ourselves, were expected to feel;
>
> 'Tis a part, I'm afraid, of a deeply laid plan
>
> To bring back the abuses of Rome if they can.
>
> And when SHE is triumphant, you'll bitterly rue
>
> That you gave up that Protestant bulwark – your pew.

The clear glass windows, of uneven crown glass with bottle-glass here and there in the upper lights, will show the churchyard yews and elms and the flying clouds outside. Shafts of sunlight will fall on hatchments, those triangular-framed canvasses hung on the aisle walls and bearing the arms of noble families of the place. Over the chancel arch hang the Royal Arms, painted by some talented inn-sign artist, with a lively lion and unicorn supporting the shield in which we may see quartered the white horse of Hanover. The roofs of the church will be ceiled within for warmth, and our boxed-in pew will save us from draught. Look behind you; blocking the tower arch you will see a wooden gallery in which the choir is tuning its instruments, fiddle, base viol, serpent. And on your left in the north aisle there is a gallery crowded under the roof. On the tiers of wooden benches here sit the

Monument to the Second
Lord Sherborne by
Rysbreck 1749, St Mary
Magdalene, Sherborne
Glos.

Sir JOHN DUTTON Baronet
Son of SIR RALPH DUTTON, by MARY, Daughter of PETER BARWICK
Doctor of Physick departed this Life February the first 1742/3
in the sixty first Year of His Age
He was twice Married
First to MARY, only child of SIR RUSHOUT CULLEN of UPTON
in Warwickshire Baronet by Her having no issue
His second Wife was MARY, Daughter of FRANCIS KECK
of Great TEW, in the County of OXFORD, ESQ
By whom He had One daughter, who dyed an Infant
He represented this County in Parliament

With great Integrity
Was an excellent Justice of Peace
Hospitable, Affable, & Benevolent

charity children in their blue uniforms, within reach of the parish beadle who, in the corner of the west gallery, can admonish them with
his painted stave.

The altar is out of sight. This is because the old screen survives
across the chancel arch and its doors are locked. If you can look
through its carved woodwork, you will see that the chancel is bare
except for the memorial floor slabs and brasses of previous incum-
bents, and the elaborate marble monument upon the wall, by a noted
London sculptor, in memory of some lay-rector of the 18th century.

No choir stalls are in the chancel, no extra rich flooring. The Lord's
Table or altar is against the east wall and enclosed on three sides by
finely-turned rails such as one sees as stair balusters in a country
house. The Table itself is completely covered with a carpet of plum-
covered velvet, embroidered on its western face with IHS in golden
rays. Only on those rare occasions, once a quarter and at Easter and
Christmas and Whit Sunday when there is to be a Communion service, is the Table decked. Then indeed there will be a fair linen cloth
over the velvet, and upon the cloth a chalice, paten and two flagons all
of silver, and perhaps two lights in silver candlesticks. On Sacrament
Sundays those who are to partake of Communion will leave their box-
pews either at the Offertory Sentence (when in modern Holy
Communion services the collection is taken), or at the words 'Ye that
do truly and earnestly repent you of your sins, and are in love and
charity with your neighbours', and they will be admitted through the
screen doors to the chancel. They will have been preceded by the
incumbent. Thereafter the communicants will remain kneeling until
the end of the service, as many as can around the Communion rails,
the rest in the western side of the chancel.

The only object which will be familiar from the Victorian church is
the font, still near the entrance to the church and symbolical of the
entrance of the Christian to Christ's army. Beside the font is a large
pew whose door opens facing it. This is the christening pew and here
the baby, its parents and the god-parents wait until after the second
lesson, when the incumbent will come forward to baptise the child in
the presence of the congregation. Some churches had Churching pews
where mothers sat.

The lighting of the church is wholly by candles. In the centre of the
nave a branched brass candelabrum is suspended by two interlocking
rods painted blue, the two serpent heads which curl round and inter-
lock them being gilded. In other parts of the church, in distant box-
pews or up in the choir gallery, light is from single candles in brass
sconces fixed to the woodwork. If the chancel is dark, there may be

two fine silver candlesticks on the altar for the purpose of illumination. But candles are not often needed, for services are generally in the hours of daylight, and the usual time for a country evensong is three o'clock in the afternoon, not six or half-past six as is now the custom.

Outside the church on a sunny Sunday morning the congregation gathers. The poorer sort are lolling against the tombstones, while the richer families, also in their best clothes, move towards the porch where the churchwardens stand with staves ready to conduct them to their private pews. The farm-workers do not wear smocks for church, but knee breeches and a long coat and shoes. Women wear wooden shoes, called pattens, when it is wet, and take them off in the porch. All the men wear hats, and they hang them on pegs on the walls when they enter the church.

All this island over, there was a hush of feudal quiet in the country on a Sunday. We must sink into this quiet to understand and tolerate, with our democratic minds, the graded village hierarchy, graded by birth and occupation, by clothes and by seating in the church. The Sabbath as a day of rest and worship touched all classes. Our feeblest poets rose from bathos to sing its praises. I doubt if Felicia Hemens ever wrote better than this, in her last poem (1835), composed less than a week before she died.

> How many blessed groups this hour are bending,
> Through England's primrose meadow paths, their way
> Towards spire and tower, midst shadowy elms ascending,
> Whence the sweet chimes proclaim the hallowed day:
> The halls from old heroic ages grey
> Pour their fair children forth; and hamlets low,
> With whose thick orchard blooms the soft winds play,
> Send out their inmates in a happy flow,
> Like a freed rural stream.
>
>   I may not tread
> With them those pathways, – to the feverish bed
> Of sickness bound, – yet, O my God, I bless
> Thy mercy, that with Sabbath peace hath filled
> My chastened heart, and all its throbbings stilled
> To one deep calm of lowliest thankfulness.

Verses turned in aid of A Public Subscription (1952) towards the restoration of the Church of St Katherine, Chiselhampton, Oxon.

Across the wet November night
The church is bright with candlelight
    And waiting Evensong.
A single bell with plaintive strokes
Pleads louder than the stirring oaks
    The leafless lanes along.

It calls the choirboys from their tea
And villagers, the two or three,
    Damp down the kitchen fire,
Let out the cat, and up the lane
Go paddling through the gentle rain
    Of misty Oxfordshire.

How warm the many candles shine
On SAMUEL DOWBIGGIN's design
    For this interior neat,
These high box pews of Georgian days
Which screen us from the public gaze
    When we make answer meet;

How gracefully their shadow falls
On bold pilasters down the walls
 And on the pulpit high.
The chandeliers would twinkle gold
As pre-Tractarian sermons roll'd
 Doctrinal, sound and dry.

From that west gallery no doubt
The viol and serpent tooted out
 The Tallis tune to Ken,
And firmly at the end of prayers
The clerk below the pulpit stairs
 Would thunder out 'Amen.'

But every wand'ring thought will cease
Before the noble altarpiece
 With carven swags array'd,
For there in letters all may read
The Lord's Commandments, Prayer and Creed,
 Are decently display'd.

On country mornings sharp and clear
The penitent in faith draw near
 And kneeling here below
Partake the Heavenly Banquet spread
Of Sacramental Wine and Bread
 And Jesus' presence know.

And must that plaintive bell in vain
Plead loud along the dripping lane?
 And must the building fall?
Not while we love the Church and live
And of our charity will give
 Our much, our more, our all.

The Church in the Fifteenth Century

THE VILLAGE LOOKS DIFFERENT. The church is by far the most prominent building unless there is a manor-house, and even this is probably a smaller building than the church and more like what we now think of as an old farm. The church is so prominent because the equivalents of cottages in the village are at the grandest 'cruck houses' (that is to say tent-like buildings with roofs coming down to the ground), and most are mere hovels. They are grouped round the church and manor-house and look rather like a camp. There is far more forest everywhere, and in all but the Celtic fringes of the island agriculture is strip cultivation, that is to say the tilled land is laid out in long strips with no hedges between and is common to the whole community, as are the grazing rights in various hedged and well-watered fields. There are more sheep than any other animals in these enclosures. The approaches to the village are grassy tracks very muddy in winter. Each village is almost a country to itself.

Not only does everyone go to church on Sunday and in his best clothes; the church is used on weekdays too, for it is impossible to say daily prayers in the little hovels in which most of the villagers live. School is taught in the porch, business is carried out by the cross in the market where the booths are (for there are no shops in the village, only open stalls as in market squares today). In the nave of the church on a weekday there are probably people gossiping in some places, while in others there are people praying.

The nave of the church belonged to the people, and they used it as today we use a village hall or social club. Our new suburban churches which are used as dance halls during the week with sanctuary partitioned off until Sunday, have something in common with the medieval church. But there is this difference:in the middle ages all sport and pleasure, all plays and dancing were 'under God'. God was near, hanging on his Cross above the chancel arch, and mystically present in the sacrament in the pyx hanging over the altar beyond.

Let us go in by its new south porch to our parish church of five-hundred years ago. Many of the features which were there when we last saw it are still present, the screen and the font for instance, but the

Parish Church of the Holy Cross & Owlpen Manor, Glos

walls are now painted all over. Medieval builders were not concerned with 'taste'. But they were moved by fashion. If the next village had a new tower, they must have one like it. If the latest style at the nearest big abbey or bishop's seat made their own building seem out of date, then it must be rebuilt. At the time of which we are writing, the style would be Perpendicular. Only the most showy features of earlier building – a Norman chancel arch removed in a few instances to the south door, a 'decorated' window with rich tracery, and perhaps a column with sculptured foliage capital of Early English times – might be spared if they could be made to look well.

Where we go in, there is a stoup made of stone or metal, containing Holy Water. And somewhere near, very prominent, is the font. Over it is a painted wooden cover, rising like a church steeple and securely clasped down to the basin of the font and locked. This is because the font contains Baptismal Water, which is changed only twice a year at Easter and Whitsun when it is solemnly blessed. The cover is raised by means of a weight and pulley. The plaster walls are covered with paintings, mostly of a dull brick-red with occasional blues and greens and blacks. The older painting round any surviving Norman windows is picked out in squares to resemble masonry. Chiefly the paintings are pictures. There will be scenes in the life of Our Lady on the north wall, and opposite us probably a huge painting of St Christopher carrying Our Lord as a child on his shoulders and walking through a stream in which fishes are swimming about and fishermen hooking a few out around St Christopher's feet. It was a pious belief that whoever looked at St Christopher would be safe that day from sudden death. The belief is kept alive today on the dashboards of motor-cars. All the windows will be filled with stained glass, depicting local saints and their legends. Our Lord as a baby and receiving homage as the

Saviour will be painted somewhere on the walls. But chiefly there will be pictures and images of Our Lady, who will probably be portrayed more often in the church than her Son. Our Lady was the favourite saint of England, and more old churches are dedicated to her than to anyone else. The Christianity of late medieval England was much concerned with Our Lord as Saviour and Man, and with Our Lady as His mother.

The wooden chancel roofs will all have painted beams, red, green, white and gold and blue. The nave roof may not be painted but over the rood-beam just above the chancel arch it will be more richly carved and painted than elsewhere. The stone floor of the church is often covered with yew boughs or sweet-smelling herbs whose aroma is stronger when crushed underfoot. Strong smells were a feature of medieval life. People did not wash much or change their clothes often, and the stink of middens must have made villages unpleasant places in hot weather. Crushed yew and rosemary must have been a welcome contrast in the cool brightness of the church. Five-hundred years ago, most churches had a few wooden benches in the nave. In some districts, notably Devon, Cornwall and parts of East Anglia, these were elaborately carved. In most places they were plain seats of thick pieces of oak. People often sat along the stone ledges on the wall or on the bases of the pillars. And the pillars of the nave had stone or wooden brackets with statues of saints standing on them.

And here in the nave, the people's part of the church, we have not yet looked eastward to Our Lord upon the Cross. His figure hanging on a wooden cross over the chancel arch, with St Mary and St John weeping on either side of Him at the foot of the cross, looks down from above the screen. This dominates the nave, and behind it or above it, painted on the east wall, is the depiction of the Doom. There, above His Body on the Rood, is a painting of the Resurrected Christ, the severe judge. His wounds are shown, His hands are raised with the nail prints in them, and His eyes fix you as you stare up. Angels blow trumpets around Him, and there rising from their graves are naked souls, painted as naked bodies but wearing head-dresses, tiaras, crowns and mitres to show their rank in life. On one side they enter rather joylessly the gates of heaven. On the other, with terrible imagery, are shewn devils with sharks' teeth and rolling eyes, hauling off the helpless souls to the gaping mouth of hell, a yawning cauldron in the bottom corner of the picture. The artists had a far more enjoyable time drawing devils and hell than angels and heaven. For one sweet-faced saint or tender portrait of Our Lady surviving in the wall-painting in our islands, there must be two or three alarming devils.

Heaven is represented in the chancel beyond that richly-painted screen, where the priest murmurs scarcely audible Latin and where the Body of Our Lord under the form of bread, hangs above the altar in a shrouded pyx. Much chatting goes on in the church during sermon and Mass, and we may now approach the screen to examine it and the jewel-like blazing richness beyond, in the holiest part of the church.

Through the screen which runs across the whole width of the church, you may glimpse the richest part of all this teaching imagery. The altars at the end of the aisles are either guild chapels, or family chapels, each with their paid priests. The Shoemakers may have an altar dedicated to Crispin, and will subscribe for its upkeep and to keep its lights burning. Another chapel may be kept up by a guild which pays a priest to say Mass for the Souls of its departed members. The secular descendants of these guilds are the trade unions and burial societies of today. The big town churches such as those at Coventry, Stamford and Bristol, had many guild chapels with priests maintained to serve them. And many altars contained a relic of a saint. The walls round the altars were painted, the roofs above them were richer and more elaborately painted than those in the people's part of the church, the altar hangings were of the richest silks and threaded with jewels, the fair linen-cloth laid upon the altar itself a white, plain contrast

The FONT, Burford Church, OXON

with the elaborate hangings. The floors of the chancel are of marble or tiles. Brasses of dead priests shone bright among them. You may see what they looked like in illuminated missals. The ornaments on the altar were few, candles perhaps, and if a cross, then a small one to help the priest in his devotions – for here in the chancel we meet the risen Lord. Only in the nave is He dead on the cross, as large as life.

Few people will make their communion at Mass. Indeed it is rare for anyone to make his communion except at Easter. People think of the Mass as something offered for them rather than something of which they partake the sacred elements.

On a hot summer Sunday morning in the country, when I have been reading Chaucer to the sound of bells pouring through the trees, I have been able dimly to imagine this late medieval religion. Life is short for everybody. It is matter of fact. The pictures on the church walls are not thought of as 'art', but are there to tell a story. Small parish churches were not consciously made beautiful. They were built and decorated for effect, to be better than the church in the next village, to be the best building in the village itself, for it is the House of God, and God become Man – that was the great discovery – offered here upon the altar. All sorts of miraculous stories were invented about Him, and even more about His mother. Because He was Man born of woman, he becomes within the grasp of everyone. Few of the extravagances of German and Spanish late medieval art are found in English representations of the scourging, the crucifixion and the deposition. Jesus is thought of as the baby of poor people who received the tributes of a king. His mother is the most beautiful woman in the world – and how many lovely, loving faces of Our Lady we may see in the old glass, wall-paintings and statues which survive in England. And she bore a Spotless Son who was God and Judge of all. No wonder she was loved by the pious English.

The miracles of Our Lord were not so interesting to these peoples as the miracles they ascribed to His saints. Here extravagancy knew no bounds. St Petroc sailed in a silver bowl from Cornwall to an isle in the Indian Ocean. St Winifred was beheaded by an angry lover, but her head was reunited to her body and she became an abbess. There were saints like St Quintin who cured dropsy, saints for toothache, and for colds and fever, and for finding things. There were patron saints for every craft and trade. There were miraculous images which winked, or flew to bedsides; there were statues of saints that had never been, like the Maid Uncumber in old St Paul's Cathedral.

Though for the everyday things of life there were friendly saints who helped, life itself must have been terrifying, a continual rush to

44

escape hell. Our Lord and His Mother were the loving and human part of it; hell was the terrifying part. The Devil was seen. His fellow devils yawned as gargoyles with bats' wings on the north walls of the church, black against the evening sky. The white teeth of devils and their red eyes gleamed out of the darkness. Evil spirits lurked behind stones on lonely moors and ranged the deep woods. Good and evil fought together in the roar of the storm. All thought, all sight, every breath of the body, was under God. The leaping sciapod, the man-eating mantichora, the unicorn, might easily be met in the forest by men with imaginations, which as easily would expect to see Our Lady flying through the air, or the local saint, for centuries enshrined in his altar, walking down the street. The witch cast her evil spells, blood and death lay around everywhere, the entrails of a man hung, drawn and quartered, shone black with flies in the sun, silvery lepers tinkled their bells, creating loneliness around them. The fear that men felt is expressed in the grotesque carvings over the north walls of churches, and in the corbels and bosses of roofs, and in bench-ends, screens and miserere stalls. Their humour is shown there too. Chiefly in the figure of Our Lady do we see the tenderness and sweetness of this late religion.

So when we walk down a green lane like an ancient cart track towards the ringing church-bells, we can see the power of God in the blossom and trees, remember legends of the saints about birds and stones, and recall miracles that happened in the parish at this or that spot. And on a feast day we can see the churchyard set out with tables for the church ale when mass is over, and as we enter the nave we can see it thronged below the painted roof and walls with people in the village, young and old, and the rest of the parish crowding in with us.

Saxon Church of St Laurence,
Bradford-on-Avon, Wilts.

The Church Before The Fifteenth Century

There was a christian church in the Roman settlement at Silchester, Berkshire, and its remains have been excavated. It had an apse at the west end instead of the east where one would expect it to be, and the altar which is supposed to have been wooden and square, was also in the west. The form of worship was probably more like that of the Orthodox church today than the western rite.

But there are enough later pre-Conquest churches remaining to give us an idea of the architecture of those times. There are two types. The southern, of which the earliest churches are found in Kent – three in Canterbury, St Mary Lyminge, Reculver, and, most complete, Bradwell, Essex, all of which are 7th century – were the result of the Italian mission of St Augustine, and were reinforced after the coming of St Theodore in 669. In plan and style they resembled certain early Italian churches. The northern group found in Northumberland and Durham are survivals of the Celtic church. Their architecture is said to have come from Gaul, and is more barbaric looking.

In the northern group, the most complete is Escombe, Durham (7th and early 8th century?), a stern building, nave and chancel only, with squared rubble walls, small windows high up and square or round headed, and a narrow and tall rounded chancel arch. We have a picture of the interiors of these northern churches from near contemporary accounts. The walls and capitals and arch of the sanctuary were adorned 'with designs and images and many sculptured figures in relief on the stone and pictures with a pleasing variety of colours and a wonderful charm'. We learn, too, of purple hangings and gold and silver ornaments with precious stones.

Elsewhere in England the most considerable remains of pre-Conquest work are those at Monkwearmouth (Durham), Jarrow (Durham), Brixworth (Northants), Deerhurst (Glos), Bradford-on-Avon (Wilts.), the tower of Earls Barton (Northants), Barton-on-Humber (Lincs), Sompting (Sussex), the Crypts at Repton (Derby), Wing (Bucks), and Hexham (Northumberland). From pre-Conquest sculpture, like the moving relief of the Harrowing of Hell in Bristol Cathedral, and from such enrichment as survives in such objects as St

47

Cuthbert's stole (Durham), the Alfred Jewel in the Ashmolean Museum, Oxford, the beautiful drawing in the Winchester Psalter and Lindisfarne Gospel in the British Museum, we know that these Romanesque masons, sculptors and illuminators were very fine artists, as fine as there have ever been in England.

However, it is safer to try to imagine our parish church as it was in Norman times, as far more of our old churches are known to be Norman in origin than pre-Conquest, even though as in the church of Kilpeck (Herefordshire) the pre-Conquest style of decoration may have continued into Norman times. It is narrow and stone built. Let us suppose it divided into three parts. The small, eastward chancel is either square-ended or apsidal. Then comes the tower supported internally on round arches. The nave, west of the low tower, is longer than the chancel. The windows are small and high up. The church is almost like a fortress outside. And it is indeed a fortress of Christianity in a community where pagan memories and practices survive, where barons are like warring kings and monasteries are the centres of faith. These small village churches are like mission churches in a jungle clearing.

There are no porches, and we enter the building by doors to the nave on the north, south or west. Inside, the walls of the nave are painted with red lines to look like blocks of stone. The roof is hidden by a flat wooden ceiling painted with lozenges. The floor of the nave is paved with small blocks of stone or with red tiles. There are no pews. We can only see the chancel through a richly moulded round arch, that very arch which is now the South Door of your parish church. Above this chancel arch is a painted Doom, not so terrifying as that of the 15th-century church, for all the painting here is in the manner of the mosaics still seen in basilicas of Italy and eastern Europe.

The splays of the windows in the nave have figures of saints painted on them. But it is through the chancel that we see the greatest riches. Stained glass is rare. If there is any it is in the sanctuary and black with much leading and giving the impression of transparent mosaics. The walls are painted with figures, also recalling mosaic pictures. There are bands of classic style, patterns dividing them. The altar is of stone, small and box-like, recalling the tombs of Christians in the catacombs of Rome in the earliest days of Christianity. The altar stands well away from the eastern, semi-circular end of the apse. It is covered with a cloth hanging over its four sides, decorated with vertical bands.

Our Lord is depicted on the cross as a King and Judge, not as a man in anguish as in later crucifixions. The religion of the time was less concerned with Him and Our Lady as human beings, more concerned with the facts of Judgement, Death and Hell. It was more ascetic and severe.

Saxon Crypt,
St Wystan's, Repton,
Derbyshire

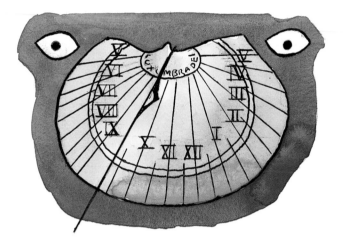

Septuagesima

Septuagesima – seventy days
To Easter's primrose tide of praise;
The Gesimas – Septua, Sexa, Quinc
Mean Lent is near, which makes you think.
Septuagesima – when we're told
To 'run the race', to 'keep our hold',
Ignore injustice, not give in,
And practise stern self-discipline;
A somewhat unattractive time
Which hardly lends itself to rhyme.

    But still it gives the chance to me
To praise our dear old C. of E.
So other Churches please forgive
Lines on the Church in which I live,
The Church of England of my birth,
The kindest Church to me on earth.
There may be those who like things fully
Argued out, and call you 'woolly';
Ignoring Creeds and Catechism
They say the C. of E.'s 'in schism'.
There may be those who much resent
Priest, Liturgy, and Sacrament,

Whose worship is what they call 'free',
Well, let them be so, but for me
There's refuge in the C. of E.
And when it comes that I must die
I hope the Vicar's standing by,
I won't care if he's 'Low' or 'High'
For he'll be there to aid my soul
On that dread journey to its goal,
With Sacrament and prayer and Blessing
After I've done my last confessing.
And at that time may I receive
The Grace most firmly to believe,
For if the Christian's Faith's untrue
What is the point of me and you?
    But this is all anticipating
Septuagesima – time of waiting,
Running the race or holding fast.
Let's praise the man who goes to light
The church stove on an icy night.
Let's praise that hard-worked he or she
The Treasurer of the P.C.C.
Let's praise the cleaner of the aisles,
The nave and candlesticks and tiles.
Let's praise the organist who tries
To make the choir increase in size,
Or if that simply cannot be,
Just to improve its quality.
Let's praise the ringers in the tower
Who come to ring in cold and shower.
But most of all let's praise the few
Who are seen in their accustomed pew
Throughout the year, whate'er the weather,
That they may worship God together.
These, like a fire of glowing coals,
Strike warmth into each other's souls,
And though they be but two or three
They keep the Church for you and me.

Diary of a Church Mouse

Here among long-discarded cassocks,
Damp stools, and half-split open hassocks,
Here where the Vicar never looks
I nibble through old service books.
Lean and alone I spend my days
Behind this Church of England baize.
I share my dark forgotten room
With two oil-lamps and half a broom.
The cleaner never bothers me,
So here I eat my frugal tea.
My bread is sawdust mixed with straw;
My jam is polish for the floor.

Christmas and Easter may be feasts
For congregations and for priests,
And so may Whitsun. All the same,
They do not fill my meagre frame.
For me the only feast at all
Is Autumn's Harvest Festival,
When I can satisfy my want
With ears of corn around the font.
I climb the eagle's brazen head
To burrow through a loaf of bread.
I scramble up the pulpit stair
And gnaw the marrows hanging there

It is enjoyable to taste
These items ere they go to waste,
But how annoying when one finds
That other mice with pagan minds
Come into church my food to share
Who have no proper business there.

Two field mice who have no desire
To be baptized, invade the choir.
A large and most unfriendly rat
Comes in to see what we are at.
He says he thinks there is no God
And yet he comes . . . it's rather odd.
This year he stole a sheaf of wheat
(It screened our special preacher's seat),
And prosperous mice from fields away
Come in to hear the organ play,
And under cover of its notes
Ate through the altar's sheaf of oats.
A Low Church mouse, who thinks that I
Am too papistical, and High,
Yet somehow doesn't think it wrong
To munch through Harvest Evensong,
While I, who starve the whole year through,
Must share my food with rodents who
Except at this time of the year
Not once inside the church appear.

   Within the human world I know
Such goings-on could not be so,
For human beings only do
What their religion tells them to.
They read the Bible every day
And always, night and morning, pray,
And just like me, the good church mouse,
Worship each week in God's own house,
   But all the same it's strange to me
How very full the church can be
With people I don't see at all
Except at Harvest Festival.

Christmas

The bells of waiting Advent ring,
    The Tortoise stove is lit again
And lamp-oil light across the night
    Has caught the streaks of winter rain
In many a stained-glass window sheen
From Crimson Lake to Hooker's Green.

The holly in the windy hedge
    And round the Manor House the yew
Will soon be stripped to deck the ledge,
    The altar, font and arch and pew,
So that the villagers can say
'The church looks nice' on Christmas Day.

Provincial public houses blaze
    And Corporation tramcars clang,
On lighted tenements I gaze
    Where paper decorations hang,
And bunting in the red Town Hall
Says 'Merry Christmas to you all.'

And London shops on Christmas Eve
    Are strung with silver bells and flowers
As hurrying clerks the City leave
    To pigeon-haunted classic towers,
And marbled clouds go scudding by
The many-steepled London sky.

And girls in slacks remember Dad,
    And oafish louts remember Mum,
And sleepless children's hearts are glad,
    And Christmas-morning bells say 'Come!'
Even to shining ones who dwell
Safe in the Dorchester Hotel.

And is it true? And is it true,
    This most tremendous tale of all,
Seen in a stained-glass window's hue,
    A Baby in an ox's stall?
The Maker of the stars and sea
Become a Child on earth for me?

And is it true? For if it is,
    No loving fingers tying strings
Around those tissued fripperies,
    The sweet and silly Christmas things,
Bath salts and inexpensive scent
And hideous tie so kindly meant,

No love that in a family dwells,
    No carolling in frosty air,
Nor all the steeple-shaking bells
    Can with this single Truth compare –
That God was Man in Palestine
And lives today in Bread and Wine.

THE NEWER CHURCHES

O F THE 16,000 PARISH churches in England more than half have been built since the 17th century, and the majority of these were erected in the last and present centuries.

In fact some of the noblest churches are post-Reformation, from cathedrals like St. Paul's and Truro and Liverpool, to the great town churches designed by such architects as Hawksmoor, Gibbs, Street, Butterfield, Pearson, Brooks, Bodley, Nicholson and Comper.

Usually the plan was of nave with three-decker pulpit dominating for Mattins, Litany and Evensong, a screen through which the congregation passed for Communion, and a Baptistry at the west end. The earliest post-Reformation churches usually had west galleries for organ and choir and also side galleries, because by the 17th century the population had begun to increase, especially in the towns where many new churches were built. The churches of the 17th and 18th centuries were mostly built on the English medieval plan. The only noticeable new feature in the more traditional churches was that the chancels were shallower and broader than those surviving from earlier times.

The style of tracery and decoration and wood-carving certainly changed. Windows were square-headed in the 16th century, and thereafter became round-headed. Grapes and cherubs and a cornucopia of fruit cascaded down the sides of altar-pieces, wreathed round the panelling of pulpits, and flattened themselves into patterns on the ceiling. The Renaissance style of Italy became the fashion. But it was an English version. Wren's Portland stone steeples and lead spires, so happily clustering round St. Paul's Cathedral, are a recollection of Gothic architecture, though most of them are Renaissance in detail.

From the middle of the 18th century until its end, new churches were Classic, usually in the manner of the Brothers Adam, with chaste decorations in low relief in interior plaster and woodwork, and comparatively plain exteriors.

But Gothic never died. The style was driven by the Renaissance out of churches and houses into barns, farms and cottages. It was revived in a romantic form, suggesting Strawberry Hill (1733), even in the 17th century. And a slender case might be made for its never having died even in ecclesiastical building. There are Stuart churches which are Tudor Gothic, such as Low Ham in Somerset (1624), and Staunton

Duke of Wellington Monument, St Paul's

Harald in Leicestershire (1653), which are like late Perpendicular medieval churches, and not a conscious revival but a continuance of the old style. St Martins in the Fields, London, until its rebuilding by Gibbs in 1721, had been continuously rebuilt in the Gothic style since the time of Henry VIII.

In the reign of Queen Anne Parliament passed an act to remedy the insufficiency of accommodation for worship in London and the vicinity. Leading architects of the time like James Gibbs, Archer and Hawksmoor were employed, and several fine churches which challenge those of Wren were the result. Other large towns, for this was a time when the population of the Midlands was rapidly expanding, followed London's example.

Another reason for the erection of new churches in the 18th century was the inadequacy of medieval buildings. They could sometimes hold galleries erected in the aisles and at the west end, but no more. Old prints show us town churches which have almost the appearance of an opera house, galleries projecting beyond galleries, with the charity children away up in the top lighted by dormers in the roof, pews all over the aisles and in the chancel, and only here and there a pointed arch or a bit of window tracery to show that this was once a gothic medieval church. Walls began to bulge, stone decayed, structures were unsound and ill-behaved children could not be seen by the beadle and clerk. The only thing to do was to pull down the building. A surviving interior of this sort is the parish church of Whitby. To go into it is like entering the hold of a ship. There are box-pews shoulder high in all directions, galleries, private pews, and even a pew over the chancel screen. Picturesque and beautiful as it is, with the different colours of baize lining the pews, and the splendid joinery of varying dates, such an uneven effect cannot have pleased the 18th-century man of taste. Therefore when they became overloaded with pews, these old churches were taken down and new ones in Classic or Strawberry Hill Gothic style were erected on the sites.

In the country there can have been little need to rebuild the old church on the grounds of lack of accommodation. Here rebuilding was done at the dictates of taste. A landlord might find the church too near his house, or sited wrongly for a landscape improvement he was contemplating in the park, or he might simply dislike the old church on aesthetic grounds as a higgledy-piggledy, barbarous building. Most counties in England have more than one 18th-century church, now a sad relic in a park devastated by timber merchants, still crowning some rise or looking like a bit of Italy or ancient Greece in the pastoral English landscape. Pointed windows, pinnacled towers and

Christ Church and Rectory, Spitalfields, London

battlemented walls were considered ecclesiastical and picturesque. They went with sham ruins and amateur antiquarianism, then coming into fashion. The details of these Gothic churches were not correct according to ancient examples. Nor do I think they were intended to be. Their designers strove after a picturesque effect, not antiquarian copying. The interiors were embellished with Chippendale Gothic woodwork and plaster-work. Again nothing was 'correct'. Who had ever heard of a medieval box-pew or an ancient ceiling that was plaster moulded? The Gothic taste was but plaster deep, concerned with a decorative effect and not with structure. The supreme example of this sort of church is Shobdon, Herefordshire (1753).

Amid all this concern with taste, industrialism comes upon us. It was all very well for the squire to fritter away his time with matters of taste in his country park, all very well for Boulton and Watt to try to harness taste to their iron-works at Soho, as Darby before them had

All Saints, Margaret Street
London W1

tried at Ironbridge; the mills of the midlands and the north were rising. Pale mechanics, slave-driven children and pregnant women were working in the new factories. The more intelligent villagers were leaving for the towns where there was more money to be made. From that time until the present day, the country has been steadily drained of its best people. Living in hovels, working in a rattling twilight of machines, the people multiplied. Ebenezer Elliott the Corn Law Rhymer (1781–1849) was their poet:

> *When wilt thou save the People?*
>   *O God of mercy, when?*
> *The people, Lord, the people,*
>   *Not thrones and crowns, but men!*
> *Flowers of thy heart, O God, are they;*
> *Let them not pass, like weeds, away –*
> *Their heritage a sunless day.*
>   *God save the people!*

The composition of this poem was a little later than the Million Act of 1818, by which Parliament voted one million pounds towards the building of churches in new districts. The sentiments of the promoters of the Bill cannot have been so unlike those of Elliott. Less charitable hearts, no doubt, terrified by the atheism consequent on the French Revolution and apprehensive of losses to landed proprietors, regarded the Million Act as a thank-offering to God for defending them from French free-thinking and continental economics. Others saw in these churches bulwarks against the rising tide of Dissent. Nearly three hundred new churches were built in industrial areas between 1819 and 1830. The Lords Commissioner of the Treasury who administered the fund required them to be built in the most economical mode, 'with a view to accommodating the greatest number of persons at the smallest expense within the compass of an ordinary voice, one half of the number to be free seats for the poor'.

One can visualise a Commissioners' Church as it was first built, by piecing together the various undisturbed parts of these churches in different towns. The Gothic was a matter of decoration, except in St. Luke's new church, Chelsea, London, and not of construction. A Commissioners' Church will be found in that part of a town where streets have names like Nelson Crescent, Adelaide Place, Regent

Square, Brunswick Terrace and Hanover Villas. The streets round it will have the spaciousness of Georgian speculative building, low-terraced houses in brick or stucco with fanlights over the doors, and, until the pernicious campaign against Georgian railings during the Nazi war, there were pleasant cast-iron verandahs on the first floor and simple railings round the planted square. Out of a wide paved space, railed in with Greek or Gothic cast iron according to the style of the building, will rise the Commissioners' Church, a brick structure with Bath stone dressings, two rows of windows and a noble entrance portico at the west end. Such churches are generally locked today, for the neighbourhood has often 'gone down'; the genteel late Georgian families who lived there moved into arboured suburbs at the beginning of this century, and their houses have been sub-let in furnished rooms.

By 1850 began a great period of English church building, which is comparable with the 15th century. Much as we regret the Victorian architect's usual 'restoration' of an old building, when he came to design a new one, he could produce work which was often original and awe-inspiring. To name only a few London churches, All Saints', Margaret Street; St Augustine's, Kilburn; St James the Less, Victoria; St Columba's, Haggerston; Holy Trinity, Sloane Street; Holy Redeemer, Clerkenwell; St Michael's, Camden Town; and St Cyprian's, Clarence Gate, are some large examples of the period which have survived Prussian bombing.

Already by the 1840s architects were attaching moral properties to Gothic styles. Since Gothic was the perfect style, what was the perfect style of Gothic? I do not know who it was who started the theory that early Gothic is crude, middle is perfection, and late is debased. But – certainly from the middle of the 1840s, this theory was held by most of the rising young church architects.

This is the reason why in mid-Victorian suburbs, while speculative builders were still erecting Italianate stucco mansions, in the last stuccoed gasp of the Georgian classic tradition – South Kensington and Pimlico in London are examples – the spire of Ketton or Louth soars above the chimney-pots, and a sudden break in the Palladian plaster terraces shows the irregular stone front, gabled porch and curvilinear tracery of a church in the Decorated style.

The most famous copyist was Gilbert Scott. There is no doubt of Scott's passionate affection for Gothic architecture. He pays a handsome tribute to Pugin's influence on his mind: 'Pugin's articles excited me almost to fury, and I suddenly found myself like a person awakened from a long, feverish dream, which had rendered him

66

St James the Less, Victoria, London SW1

unconscious of what was going on about him.' Scott realised some of Pugin's dreams for him. But he never did more. He was at heart a copyist and not a thinker in Gothic. The chief of those architects who 'thought in Gothic' are listed below.

William Butterfield (1814–1900) was the most severe and interesting of them. He first startled the world in 1849 with his design for All Saints', Margaret Street, London. All Saints' embodies architectural theories which Butterfield employed in most of his other churches throughout his long life. It is constructed of the material which builders in the district were accustomed to use, which in London at that time was brick. Since bricks do not lend themselves to the carving which is expected of a Gothic building, Butterfield varied his flat brick surfaces with bands of colour, both within and without. In those days the erroneous impression prevailed that Gothic decoration grew more elaborate the higher it was on a building. The patterns of bricks in Butterfield's buildings grew, therefore, more diversified and frequent towards the tops of walls, towers and steeples. The high altar is visible from every part of the church. Butterfield disapproved of side altars and never made provision for them in his churches. The chancel is the richest part of the building, and the chancel arch, higher than the arcades of the nave, gives it an effect of greater loftiness than it possesses. There is, of course, no screen. The other prominent feature of any Butterfield church is the font. That sentence in the Catechism on the number of Sacraments, 'Two only, as generally necessary to salvation, that is to say Baptism, and the Supper of the Lord', is almost spoken aloud by a Butterfield church; altar and font are the chief things we see. But when we look up at arches and roofs, we see Butterfield the builder with his delight in construction. His roofs are described by that fine writer Sir John Summerson as 'like huge, ingenious toys'. The phrase is as memorable as all Butterfield's roofs, of which the ingenuity and variety seem to have been the only sportiveness he permitted himself.

In person Butterfield was a silent, forbidding man who looked like Mr. Gladstone. He was an earnest Tractarian with a horror of everything outside the liturgy of the Book of Common Prayer. He supplied no attractive drawings to tempt clients. He was a strong disciplinarian in his office, and on the building site, scaffolding and ladders had to be dusted before he ascended to see the work in progress. He was averse to all publicity and show, and had little to do with any other architects. People had to take Butterfield or leave him. And so must we. Yet no one who has an eye for plan, construction and that sense of proportion which is the essential of all good architecture, can see a

St Augustine, Kilburn PK Road London NW6

Butterfield church without being compelled to admire it, even if he cannot like it.

The churches built by George Edmund Street, R.A. (1824–81), in the late 'fifties and throughout the 'sixties, often with schools and parsonages alongside them, are, like his character, straightforward and convinced. They are shorn of those 'picturesque' details beloved of the usual run of architects of the time. The plan of Street's buildings is immediately apparent from the exterior. His churches are built on the same principles as those of Butterfield, one altar only, and that visible from all parts of the church, a rich east end, and much westward light into the nave. Street had a sure sense of proportion, very much his own; his work, whether it is a lectern or a pulpit or a spire, is massive, and there is nothing mean about it nor over-decorated. This massive quality of his work made Street a bad restorer of old buildings, for he would boldly pull down a chancel and rebuild it in his own style. He was a great enthusiast for the arts and crafts. With his own hands he is said to have made the wooden staircase for West Challow Vicarage in Berkshire.

Street was an able sketcher of architecture, and clearly a man who could fire his pupils with his own enthusiasm, even though he never allowed those pupils a free hand in design, doing everything down to the smallest details himself.

The third of the great mid-Victorian church builders was John Loughborough Pearson (1817–97). His later buildings are of all Victorian churches those we like best today. He was, like Street and Butterfield, a Tractarian. Before designing a building he gave himself to prayer and receiving the Sacrament. The Pearson style was an Early English Gothic with deep mouldings and sharply-pointed arches; brick was usually employed for walls and vaulting, stone for trouble with skyline, and his spires, flèches and roofs form beautiful groups from any angle.

One more individualistic Gothic revivalist was William Burges (1827–81), who was as much a domestic architect and a furniture designer as an ecclesiastical man. He delighted in colour and quaintness, but being the son of an engineer, his work had a solidity of structure which saved it from ostentation. His east end of Waltham Abbey and his cathedral of St. Finbar, Cork, are his most beautiful church work, though Skelton and Studley Royal, both in Yorkshire, are overpowering in their rich colour and decoration, and very original in an early French Gothic manner.

Neither Butterfield, Street, Pearson nor Burges would have thought of copying old precedents. They had styles of their own which they had devised for themselves, continuing from the medieval Gothic but not copying it.

The last quarter of the 19th century was a time when the church was concerning herself with social problems, and building many new churches in England as well as establishing dioceses abroad. Many, and often ugly, little churches were built of brick in brand new suburbs. Cathedral-like buildings, subscribed for by the pious from wealthy parishes, were built in the slums. At the back of Crockford's Clerical Directory there is an index of English parishes with the dates of their formation. If you look up an average industrial town with, say, ten churches, you will find that the majority will have been built during the last half of the 19th century. Oldest will be the parish church, probably medieval. Next there will be a late Georgian church built by the Commissioners. Then there will be three built between 1850 and 1870, three built between 1870 and 1900, and two since then, probably after the 1914 war and in new suburbs.

It is entertaining, and not completely safe, to generalise on the inner

story of the Church and its building in Victorian and later times. In, let us say, 1850, the vicar of the parish church had become a little old for active work, and left much to his curates. His churchmanship took the form mainly of support for the Establishment and hostility to Dissent. The word 'Dissenters' applied to Nonconformists always had a faint note of contempt. Methodists and Baptists were building chapels all over the rapidly growing towns. Their religion of personal experience of salvation, of hymn-singing, ejaculations of praise; the promise of a golden heaven after death as a reward for a sad life down here in the crowded misery of back streets, disease and gnawing poverty; their weekday socials and clubs which welded the membership of the chapels in a Puritan bond of teetotalism, and non-gambling, non-smoking and well-doing: these had an appeal which today is largely dispersed into the manufactured day-dreams of the cinema and the less useful social life of the dance hall and sports club. Chapels were crowded, gas-lights flamed on popular preachers, and steamy windows resounded to the cries of 'Alleluia, Jesus saves!' A simple ceremony like total immersion or Breaking of Bread was something all the tired and poor could easily understand, after their long hours of misery in gloomy mills. Above all, the Nonconformists turned people's minds and hearts to Jesus as a personal Friend of all, especially the poor. Many a pale mechanic and many a drunkard's wife could remember the very hour of the very day on which, in that street or at that meeting, or by that building, conviction came of the truth of the Gospel, that Jesus was Christ. Then with what flaming heart he or she came to the chapel, and how fervently testified to the message of salvation and cast off the old life of sin.

Beside these simple and genuine experiences of the love of Christ, the old-established Church with its system of pew rents, and set prayers and carefully-guarded sacraments, must have seemed wicked mumbo-jumbo. No wonder the old Vicar was worried about the Dissenters. His parish was increasing by thousands as the factories boomed and the ships took our merchandise across the seas, but his parishioners were not coming to church in proportion. He had no objection therefore when the new Bishop, filled with the zeal for building which seems to have filled all Victorian bishops, decided to form two new parishes out of his own, the original parish of the little village which had become a town in less than a century. The usual method was adopted. Two clergymen were licensed to start the church life of the two new districts. These men were young; one was no doubt a Tractarian; the other was perhaps fired with the Christian Socialism of Charles Kingsley and F.D. Maurice. Neither was much concerned with the establishment of churches as bulwarks against Dissenters, but rather as houses of God among ignorant Pagans, where the Gospel might be heard, the Sacraments administered, want relieved, injustice righted and ignorance dispelled. First came the mission-room, a room licensed for services in the clergyman's lodging, then there was the school, at first a room for Sunday school only, and then came the mission church made of corrugated iron. Then there was an appeal for a church school and for a permanent church. For this church the once young clergyman, now worn after ten years' work, would apply to the Incorporated Church Building Society, and to the Church Building Fund of his own diocese; he would raise money among his poor parishioners, he would give his own money (this was a time when priests were frequently men of means), and pay his own stipend as well. The site for the church would be given by a local landowner, and who knows but that some rich manufacturer whose works were in the parish would subscribe. Whatever their Churchmanship, the new parishes formed in the 'fifties generally had their own church within twenty years.

All this while the Commissioners' Church in the town, that Greek Revival building among the genteel squares where still lived the doctors, attorneys and merchants, had an Evangelical congregation and disapproved of the old 'high and dry' vicar of the parish church. The congregation and incumbent disapproved still more of the goings on of the Tractarian priest in charge of one of the two new districts. He lit two candles on the Table which he called an 'altar', at the service of the Lord's Supper he stood with his back to the congregation instead of at the north end of the Table, he wore a coloured stole over his surplice instead of a black scarf, and he did not preach in a black gown. He was worse than the Pope of Rome or almost as bad. The ignorant artisans were being turned into Roman Catholics. The pure Gospel of the Reformation must be brought to them. So a rival church was built in the Tractarian parish, financed by the Evangelical church people of the town, and from outside by many loyal Britons who throughout England, like Queen Victoria herself, were deploring the Romish tendency in the Established Church.

Many years have passed since this controversy, and the rival Evangelical fane probably has now a clergyman who always wears a surplice and sometimes a coloured stole, who has lights on the altar and faces east to celebrate Holy Communion, while the priest and congregation of the neighbouring Tractarian church, who now have incense, reservation of the Blessed Sacrament, daily mass, confessions and a High Mass on Sundays, still regard him as 'low church'.

St Saviour's, Aberdeen Park, Highbury, London, N.

With oh such peculiar branching and over-reaching of wire
    Trolley-bus standards pick their threads from the London sky
Diminishing up the perspective, Highbury-bound retire
    Threads and buses and standards with plane trees volleying by
And, more peculiar still, that ever-increasing spire
    Bulges over the housetops, polychromatic and high.

Stop the trolley-bus, stop! And here, where the roads unite
    Of weariest worn-out London – no cigarettes, no beer,
No repairs undertaken, nothing in stock – alight;
    For over the waste of willow-herb, look at her, sailing clear,
A great Victorian church, tall, unbroken and bright
    In a sun that's setting in Willesden and saturating us here.

These were the streets my parents knew when they loved and won –
    The brougham that crunched the gravel, the laurel-girt paths that
                                             wind,
Geranium-beds for the lawn, Venetian blinds for the sun,
    A separate tradesman's entrance, straw in the mews behind,
Just in the four-mile radius where hackney carriages run,
    Solid Italianate houses for the solid commercial mind.

These were the streets they knew; and I, by descent, belong
    To these tall neglected houses divided into flats.
Only the church remains, where carriages used to throng
    And my mother stepped out in flounces and my father stepped out
                                             in spats
To shadowy stained-glass matins or gas-lit evensong
    And back in a country quiet with doffing of chimney hats.

St Saviour's, Highbury, London N5

Great red church of my parents, cruciform crossing they knew –
    Over these same encaustics they and their parents trod
Bound through a red-brick transept for a once familiar pew
    Where the organ set them singing and the sermon let them nod
And up this coloured brickwork the same long shadows grew
    As these in the stencilled chancel where I kneel in the presence of
                                         God.

Wonder beyond Time's wonders, that Bread so white and small
    Veiled in golden curtains, too mighty for men to see,
Is the Power that sends the shadows up this polychrome wall,
    Is God who created the present, the chain-smoking millions and me;
Beyond the throb of the engines is the throbbing heart of all –
    Christ, at this Highbury altar, I offer myself to Thee.

Undenominational

Undenominational
    But still the church of God
He stood in his conventicle
    And ruled it with a rod.

Undenominational
    The walls around him rose,
The lamps within their brackets shook
    To hear the hymns he chose.

'Glory' 'Gopsal' 'Russell Place'
    'Wrestling Jacob' 'Rock'
'Saffron Walden' 'Safe at Home'
    'Dorking' 'Plymouth Dock'

I slipped about the chalky lane
    That runs without the park,
I saw the lone conventicle
    A beacon in the dark.

Revival ran along the hedge
    And made my spirit whole
When steam was on the window panes
    And glory in my soul.

St Endellion

St Endellian

SAINT ENDELLION! SAINT ENDELLION! The name is like a ring of bells. I travelled late one summer evening to Cornwall in a motor car. The road was growing familiar, Delabole with its slate quarry passed, then Pendogget. Gateways in the high fern-stuffed hedges showed sudden glimpses of the sea. Port Isaac Bay with its sweep of shadowy cliffs stretched all along to Tintagel. The wrinkled Atlantic Ocean had the evening light upon it. The stone and granite manor house of Tresungers with its tower and battlements was tucked away out of the wind on the slope of a valley and there on the top of the hill was the old church of St Endellion. It looked, and still looks, just like a hare. The ears are the pinnacles of the tower and the rest of the hare, the church, crouches among wind-slashed firs.

On that evening the light bells with their sweet tone were being rung for practice. They were ringing rounds on all six bells. But as we drew near the tower – a grand, granite, fifteenth-century tower looking across half Cornwall – as we climbed the hill the bells sounded louder even than the car. 'St Endellion! St Endellion!' they seemed to

78

say. 'St Endellion' their music was scattered from the rough lichened openings over foxgloves, over grey slate roofs, lonely farms and feathery tamarisks, down to that cluster of whitewashed houses known as Trelights, the only village in the parish, and to Roscarrock and Trehaverock and Trefreock, heard perhaps, if the wind was right, where lanes run steep and narrow to that ruined, forgotten fishing place of Port Quin, 'St Endellion!'. But who was St Endellion? She was a sixth-century Celtic saint, daughter of a Welsh king, who with her sisters Minver and Teath and many other holy relations came to North Cornwall with the Gospel.

There was an Elizabethan writer who lived in the parish, Nicholas Roscárrock. He loved the old religion and was imprisoned in the Tower and put on the rack and then imprisoned again. He wrote the life of his parish saint. 'St Endelient' he called her and said she lived only on the milk of a cow:

> which cowe the lord of Trenteny kild as she strayed into his grounds; and as olde people speaking by tradition, doe report, she had a great man to her godfather, which they also say was King Arthure, whoe took the killing of the cowe in such sort, as he killed or caus'd the Man to be slaine, whom she miraculously revived.

When she was dying Endelient asked her friends to lay her dead body on a sledge and to bury her where certain young Scots bullocks or calves of a year old should of their own accord draw her. This they did and the Scots bullocks drew the body up to the windy hilltop where the church now stands.

The churchyard is a forest of upright Delabole slate headstones, a rich grey-blue stone, inscribed with epitaphs – the art of engraving lettering on slate continued in this district into the present century – names and rhymes set out on the stone spaciously, letters delicate and beautiful. From the outside it's the usual Cornish church – a long low building of elvan stone, most of it built in Tudor times. But the tower is extra special. It is of huge blocks of granite brought, they say, from Lundy Island. The ground stage of the tower is strongly moulded but the builders seem to have grown tired and to have taken less trouble with the detail higher up, though the blocks of granite are still enormous.

I can remember Endellion before its present restoration. There's a photograph of what it used to look like in the porch – pitchpine pews, pitchpine pulpit, swamping with their yellow shine the clustered granite columns of the aisles. Be careful as you open the door not to fall over. Three steps *down* and there it is, long and wide and light and simple with no pitchpine anywhere except a lectern. A nave and two aisles with barrel roofs carved with bosses, some of them old but most of them done twelve years ago by a local joiner, the village postman and the sculptress. The floor is slate. The walls are stone lightly plastered blueish-grey. There is no stained glass. Old oak and new oak benches, strong and firm and simple, fill, but do not crowd, the church. They do not hide the full length of these granite columns. The high altar is long and vast. At the end of the south aisle is the sculptured base of St Endelient's shrine, in a blue-black slate called Cataclewse, a boxwood among stones. The church reveals itself at once. Though at first glance it is unmysterious, its mystery grows. It is the mystery of satisfying proportion – and no, not just that, nor yet the feeling of age, for the present church is almost wholly early Tudor, not very old as churches go, nor is the loving use of local materials all to do with it. Why does St Endellion seem to go on praying when there is no one in it? The Blessed Sacrament is not reserved here, yet the building is alive.

There is something strange and exalting about this windy Cornish hill top looking over miles of distant cliffs, that cannot be put into words. I take a last look at St Endellion standing on a cliff top of this Atlantic coast. The sun turns the water into moving green. In

November weather, if the day is bright, the cliffs here are in shadow. The sun cannot rise high enough to strike them. The bracken is dead and brown, the grassy cliff tops vivid green; red berries glow in bushes. Ice cream cartons and cigarette packets left by summer visitors have been blown into crevices and soaked to pulp. The visitors are there for a season. Man's life on earth will last for seventy years perhaps. But this sea will go on swirling against these green and purple rocks for centuries. Long after we are dead it will rush up in waterfalls of whiteness that seem to hang half-way up the cliff face and then come pouring down with tons of ginger-beery foam. Yet compared with the age of these rocks, the sea's life is nothing. And even the age of rocks is nothing compared with the eternal life of man. And up there on the hill in St Endellion church, eternal man comes week by week in the Eucharist. That is the supreme mystery of all the mysteries of St Endellion.

Bodmin Moor

Sunday Afternoon Service in
St Enodoc Church, Cornwall

Come on! come on! This hillock hides the spire,
Now that one and now none. As winds about
The burnished path through lady's finger, thyme
And bright varieties of saxifrage,
So grows the tinny tenor faint or loud
And all things draw towards St Enodoc.

St Enodoc Church, Cornwall

Come on! come on! and it is five to three.

Paths, unfamiliar to golfers' brogues,
Cross the eleventh fairway broadside on
And leave the fourteenth tee for thirteenth green,
Ignoring Royal and Ancient, bound for God.

Come on! come on! no longer bare of foot,
The sole grows hot in London shoes again.
Jack Lambourne in his Sunday navy-blue
Wears tie and collar, all from Selfridge's.
There's Enid with a silly parasol,
And Graham in gray flannel with a crease
Across the middle of his coat which lay
Pressed 'neath the box of his Meccano set,
Sunday to Sunday.
                    Still Come on! come on!
The tinny tenor. Hover-flies remain
More than a moment on a ragwort bunch,
And people's passing shadows don't disturb
Red Admirals basking with their wings apart.
    A mile of sunny, empty sand away,
A mile of shallow pools and lugworm casts,
Safe, faint and surfy, laps the lowest tide.
    Even the villas have a Sunday look.
The Ransome mower's locked into the shed.
'I have a splitting headache from the sun,'
And bedroom windows flutter cheerful chintz
Where, double-aspirined, a mother sleeps;
While father in the loggia reads a book,
Large, desultory, birthday-present size,
Published with coloured plates by *Country Life*,
A Bernard Darwin on *The English Links*
Or Braid and Taylor on *The Mashie Shot.*
Come on! come on! he thinks of Monday's round –
Come on! come on! that interlocking grip!
Come on! come on! he drops into a doze –
Come on! come on! more far and far away
The children climb a final stile to church;

Electoral Roll still flapping in the porch –
Then the cool silence of St Enodoc.

   My eyes, recovering in the sudden shade,
Discern the long-known little things within –
A map of France in damp above my pew,
Grey-blue of granite in the small arcade
(Late Perp: and not a Parker specimen
But roughly hewn on windy Bodmin Moor),
The modest windows palely glazed with green,
The smooth slate floor, the rounded wooden roof,
The Norman arch, the cable-moulded font –
All have a humble and West Country look.
Oh 'drastic restoration' of the guide!
Oh three-light window by a Plymouth firm!
Absurd, truncated screen! oh sticky pews!
Embroidered altar-cloth! untended lamps!
So soaked in worship you are loved too well
For that dispassionate and critic stare
That I would use beyond the parish bounds
Biking in high-banked lanes from tower to tower
On sunny, antiquarian afternoons.

   Come on! come on! a final pull. Tom Blake
Stalks over from the bell-rope to his pew
Just as he slopes about the windy cliffs
Looking for wreckage in a likely tide,
Nor gives the Holy Table glance or nod.
A rattle as red baize is drawn aside,
Miss Rhoda Poulden pulls the tremolo,
The oboe, flute and vox humana stops;
A Village Voluntary fills the air
And ceases suddenly as it began,
Save for one oboe faintly humming on,

As slow the weary clergyman subsides
Tired with his bike-ride from the parish church.
He runs his hands once, twice, across his face
'Dearly beloved . . .' and a bumble-bee
Zooms itself free into the churchyard sun
And so my thoughts this happy Sabbathtide.

　　Where deep cliffs loom enormous, where cascade
Mesembryanthemum and stone-crop down,
Where the gull looks no larger than a lark
Hung midway twixt the cliff-top and the sand,
Sun-shadowed valleys roll along the sea.
Forced by the backwash, see the nearest wave
Rise to a wall of huge translucent green
And crumble into spray along the top
Blown seaward by the land-breeze. Now she breaks
And in an arch of thunder plunges down
To burst and tumble, foam on top of foam,
Criss-crossing, baffled, sucked and shot again,
A waterfall of whiteness, down a rock,
Without a source but roller's furthest reach:
And tufts of sea-pink, high and dry for years,
Are flooded out of ledges, boulders seem
No bigger than a pebble washed about
In this tremendous tide. Oh kindly slate!
To give me shelter in this crevice dry.
These shivering stalks of bent-grass, lucky plant,
Have better chance than I to last the storm.
Oh kindly slate of these unaltered cliffs,
Firm, barren substrate of our windy fields!
Oh lichened slate in walls, they knew your worth
Who raised you up to make this House of God
What faith was his, that dim, that Cornish saint,

Small rushlight of a long-forgotten church,
Who lived with God on this unfriendly shore,
Who knew He made the Atlantic and the stones
And destined seamen here to end their lives
Dashed on a rock, rolled over in the surf,
And not one hair forgotten. Now they lie
In centuries of sand beside the church.
Less pitiable are they than the corpse
Of a large golfer, only four weeks dead,
This sunlit and sea-distant afternoon.
'Praise ye the Lord ' and in another key
The Lord's name by harmonium be praised.
'The Second Evening and the Fourteenth Psalm.'

THE CHURCH OF ST PROTUS AND ST HYACINTH AT BLISLAND, CORNWALL

O F ALL THE COUNTRY churches of the West I have seen, I think that Blisland is the most beautiful. I was a boy when I first saw it, fifty or more years ago. I shall never forget that first visit to the edge of Bodmin Moor, that sweet brown home of Celtic saints, the haunted, thrilling land so full of ghosts of ancient peoples whose hut circles, beehive dwellings and burial mounds jut out above the ling and heather.

Perched on the hill above the woods stands Blisland village. It has not one ugly building in it and, what is unusual in Cornwall, the houses are round a green. Between the lichen-crusted trunks of elm and ash that grow on the green, you can see everywhere the beautiful silver-grey moorland granite. It is used for windows, for chimney stacks, for walls.

The church is down a steep slope of graveyard, past slate head-stones, and it looks over the tree-tops of a deep and elmy valley and away to the west where, like a silver shield the Atlantic sometimes shines in the sun. An opening in the churchyard wall shows a fuchsia hedge and the vicarage front door beyond. The church tower is square and weathered and made of enormous blocks of moorland granite. However did the old builders haul them to the topmost stages?

When I first saw it, the tower was stuffed with moss and with ferns which had roots here and there between the great stones, but lately it had been vilely re-pointed in hard straight lines with cement. The church itself, which seems to lean this way and that, throws out chapels and aisles in all directions. It hangs on the hillside, spotted with lichens which have softened the slates of its roof. Granite forms the tracery of its windows; a granite holy-water stoup is in the porch.

That great church architect, Sir Ninian Comper, said a church should bring you to your knees when you first enter it. Such a build-ing is Blisland. For there, before me as I open the door, is the blue-grey granite arcade, that hardest of stone to carve. One column slopes outwards as though it were going to tumble down a hill and a carved wooden beam is fixed between it and the south wall to stop it falling.

The floor is of blue slate and pale stone. Old carved benches, of dark oak, and a few chairs are the seating. The walls are white, the sun streams in through a clear west window and there, glory of glo-ries, right across the whole eastern end of the church are the richly painted screen and rood loft: all of wood.

The panels at the base of the screen are red and green. Wooden columns highly coloured, twisted like barley-sugar, burst into gilded tracery and fountain out to hold a panelled loft. There are steps to reach this loft, in the wall. Our Lord and his Mother and St John, who form the rood, are over the centre of the screen.

My eyes look up and there is the irregular old Cornish roof, shaped like the inside of an upturned ship, all its ribs richly carved, the carv-ing shown up by white plaster panels.

These old roofs, beautifully restored, are to be seen throughout the whole church. Unevenly, they stretch away beyond the screens and down the aisles. I venture in a little further.

There, through this rich screen, I can mark the blazing gold of the altars and the mediaeval style glass, some of the earliest work of Comper. Beside me in the nave is a pulpit shaped like a wine-glass, in the Georgian style and encrusted with cherubs and fruit carved in wood.

The screen, the golden altars, the stained glass and the pulpit are comparatively new. They were given by the Collins family, and designed by F. C. Eden in 1897. Eden had a vision of this old Cornish church as it was in mediaeval times. He did not do all the mediaeval things he might have done. He did not paint the walls with pictures of angels, saints and devils in amber and red.

He left the western window clear so that people in this reading age might see their books; he put in a Georgian pulpit. He centred everything on the altar to which the screen is as a golden red and green veil to the holiest mystery behind it.

In Blisland church is Norman work, there is fifteenth and sixteenth century work and there is sensitive and beautiful modern work, but chiefly it is a living church whose beauty makes you gasp, whose

The Church of ST. PROTUS & ST Hyacinth
Blisland, CORNWALL

silent peace brings you to your knees, even if you kneel on the hard
stone and slate of the floor.

St Protus and St Hyacinth, patron saints of Blisland church, pray for
me! Often in a bus or train I call to mind your lovely church, the still-
ness of that Cornish valley and the first really beautiful work of man
which my boyhood vividly remembers.

The Church of St John the Baptist at Mildenhall, Wiltshire

FEEL, UNDER YOUR FEET, an old stone floor as scrubbed and uneven as that of a farmhouse kitchen. Sniff the faint damp smell of wet earth, sweating stone, peeling plaster, dank paper, lavender, sweet william, hassocks, cassocks, candle-grease and hay – all those faint old perfumes of the past that come when one opens the leaves of a forgotten leather-bound book – when one opens the leaves and sniffs.

You are standing, in imagination, in the nave of a country church, a country church which neither the Victorians nor our own generation has touched.

There is only one in Cornwall – Launcells. In Devon I can think of West Ogwell, Branscombe, Molland. In Somerset there are Holcombe, Cameley, Swell, Sutton Mallet, Babington and a few more. In Dorset there are Eaton-on-Portland, Winterbourne Thompson, and in Wiltshire there are Inglesham and Mildenhall Bascombe.

For the moment think yourself back into this dream church. The five bells have rung down and the treble only is going. Through the old clear glass of the window, the last villagers are seen streaming along under the elms, past the limestone headstones sculptured with cherubs, hour-glasses and skulls and in at the church door.

The box pews are filling. They are so high that only the bonneted heads of the women and bowed silver locks of the men, may be seen above them. Inside, the high boxes are lined with red or green or blue baize. Outside they are painted white.

One, extra big, is the squire's pew in a special aisle all to itself. It was once the family chapel where Mass was said for the souls of the squire's ancestors – this extra-big pew has a fire-place. It is empty and the service will not begin until the squire and his lady arrive.

Look about the church for a moment while we await their arrival. White ceilings are over the chancel and nave. The walls are of plaster, washed with a pale pink or white and cream, and below the limewash you can still faintly see the traces of mediaeval wallpaintings of saints and devils with which the plaster was originally decorated. Over the chancel arch, where once hung Our Lord and Our Lady and St John, is a huge Royal Arms symbolizing the alliance of Church and State.

Noble marble slabs are on the walls, memorials of dead squires, and the effect of their carving and colour is enhanced by a wide black border painted on the plaster surface around each monument. Some of the upper lights of the clear glass windows retain pieces of old stained glass, out of reach of the hammers of Puritan reformers who delighted in smashing stained glass because they thought it a symbol of Popery.

Beside the chancel arch is a huge three-decker pulpit approached by a flight of steps. Over the pulpit hangs a sounding board. How easily it looks as though it might come crashing down on the parson's head and silence him forever. By the pulpit desk is an hour-glass in an iron stand to time the service, and below the pulpit is yet another pulpit from which the prayers and lessons will be read before the minister mounts, in his black gown and white tabs, to preach.

And below the second pulpit is a third where sits the parish clerk, who loudly says 'Amen' and leads the choir off in the metrical psalms, for this is the time before hymn-books came into general use.

A certain amount of coughing and throat clearing in the chancel indicates the presence of the Rector. That is where he dons his black gown, and, if it is Sacrament Sunday (four times a year they have a Communion service) he changes into a white surplice and black scarf.

On such special Sundays as these when all the village drains the chalice of the grapes of God in recognition of an all-serving Creator who makes the corn to grow, the birds to sing, the cows to give milk, who gives us the sweet air we breathe in this old church – on such Sacrament Sundays as these – the altar and its fair linen cloth will be decked with flagons, cup and patten and two candlesticks all of gleaming Georgian silver bright against the dark commandment

St John the Baptist, Mildenhall, Wilts

boards and richer than the rich velvet with which the altar's sides and front are draped.

Ah! There they come, the squire and his lady in through the special gate into the churchyard from the park. There is some tuning and wheezing behind us and we see high up in a gallery into the west of the church six rustics with a variety of wind instruments, a bassoon, a serpent, two oboes, a clarinet and a pitchpipe. They are the village choir and they make the melody for the psalms before the days of harmoniums and organs. Now the service will begin.

It pains me to say that in all England there are probably hardly more than a hundred churches which have survived the tampering of the last one hundred and twenty-five years. We talk of our churches as old but many are mainly Victorian in their furniture.

The west galleries are cut down; the old choir was dismissed and went disgruntled off to chapel or to form a village band or to appear self-consciously and surpliced in the chancel; the chancel was blocked by an organ or harmonium, its width was cluttered up with choir-stalls, the pulpit was removed, the plaster taken off the walls, the ceiling stripped, the high pews chopped down, the clear windows filled with coloured glass, the old floor paved with slippery and shiny brown tiles.

Of all the churches which remain untouched by the Victorians, the loveliest I know is that at Mildenhall (pronounced 'Minal') near Marlborough. It stands in the Kennet water meadows, a simple four-square affair, tower, nave and aisles either side and a chancel. When you approach it you begin to see signs of the past – clear glass panels, patched and flaking outside walls looking like an old water-colour.

And then inside you walk straight into a Jane Austen novel, into a forest of the most magnificent oak joinery, an ocean of box-pews stretching shoulder high over all the chancel. Each is carved with decorations. The doors and sides of the pews take a graceful curve either side of the font and another curve above them is made by the elegant west gallery. Norman pillars just raise their sculptured heads above the woodwork of the aisles.

It is not simply that it is an old building that makes this church so beautiful (there are thousands of old churches). It is that it contains all its Georgian fittings. Though the date is 1816, the style and quality of workmanship is that of fifty years earlier.

Mildenhall is a patriarchal church. It is the embodiment of the Church of England by law established, the still heart of England, as haunting to my memory as the tinkle of sheep bells on the Wiltshire Downs.

In Praise of the Victorians

L ET ME TAKE YOU on a church-crawl round some Victorian churches of the West. Everybody is so busy running down the Victorians or laughing at them that this is a chance to speak up in their favour.

'Ho! Ho!' says the Vicar when I go to get the key. 'You can't want to see our church. It's a Victorian monstrosity, my dear fellow', and he gives me a look which suggests that I really want the key in order to empty the offertory box.

'But I think your church is *beautiful*', I say. And he thinks I'm mad. Vicars who despise Victorian churches, church-wardens with 'artistic' leanings, advisory boards and art critics, please read these words in praise of some west country Victorians.

When they were restoring old buildings even the greatest Victorian architects were arrogant, heavy-handed and insensitive to all but some phase of Gothic architecture of which they approved. Cornish people will not willingly forgive Mr J. P. St Aubyn for his workmanlike but hideous 'restoration' of most Cornish churches. His signature is an iron footscraper by the porch. If you see that footscraper, you know J. P. St Aubyn has been at the church and there will not be much that is old left inside the building.

But when they are starting from scratch, Victorian church architects were often as original and creative and as beautiful as any who have built before or since them.

George Edmund Street (that indefatigable bearded genius who died in 1881 from overwork on building the Law Courts in London) was a brilliant artist, a scholarly and entertaining writer, the inspiring master of William Morris, Philip Webb, Norman Shaw and J. D. Sedding.

Life in Street's office was fun. One of his pupils had a stutter and could only sing without stuttering and so Morris and Webb and Shaw used to talk to him in Gregorian plainsong through rolled-up tubes of drawing-paper.

George Edmund Street designed St John's, Torquay, in 1867, for which Burne-Jones later did some pictures. He designed Holy Trinity, Barnstaple, and All Saints', Clifton, and in 1874 the superb church of Kingston in Dorset which sits so stately on a hill slope and gleams with Purbeck marble.

St James' New Church, Kingston DORSET

All Street's churches are built on rigid principles. These are they: plenty of light from the west so that people can see their books, local materials, no screen, the altar visible from all parts of the church, and every detail down to the door hinges specially designed and very practical. One of his last works was the splendid nave of Bristol Cathedral. Street's pupil J. D. Sedding designed the noble, clean and soaring church of All Saints', Falmouth in 1887.

Perhaps the most amazing church in Devon was that designed by Butterfield at Yealmpton in 1850 – a mass of local marbles like that original font he made for Ottery St Mary.

Other great Victorian churches of the west are Truro Cathedral and St Stephen's, Bournemouth, by J. L. Pearson; tall buildings those with infinite vistas of vaulted arches cutting vaulted arches. Pearson was a vista-man, vistas and vaulting.

I have always had a weakness for the late Victorian church of St David's at Exeter by W. D. Caroë. A pale green building it is, with all sorts of funny quirks in the way of stone tracery and woodwork and metal – a sort of ecclesiastical vision of the old Deller's cafe of Exeter.

Then there are Victorian churches which later architects have made more beautiful, like All Saints', Clevedon, and Wimborne St Giles, Dorset, by Sir Ninian Comper. One more I must mention, an Edwardian affair built for Lord Beauchamp by A. Randall Wells – the new church of Kempley in Gloucestershire. It is a sturdy little thing in stone with an extraordinary and enormous west window whose tracery is just a large diamond pattern in stone.

This place inside is a miniature cathedral of the arts and crafts movement: local labour was employed on it. Edward Barnsley, the Cotswold cabinet-maker, made the lectern; that fine craftsman Ernest Gimson made the candlesticks and the last surviving carver of figureheads for the old clippers carved the figures of Our Lord, St Mary and St John on the beam.

The woodwork itself in the church was painted by villagers in vermilion, ruby, golden ochre, yellow chrome, green and blue. From Yealmpton to Kempley these churches of another generation are arresting in the extreme. They are not copies of mediaeval, they are thinking in Gothic.

They are original, violent, surprising. They take some getting used to, but they are full of thought and care and were inspired by the faith of those architects and builders. There is nothing tame or mediocre about them. Go and have a look at some of those I have mentioned, if you happen to be near them.

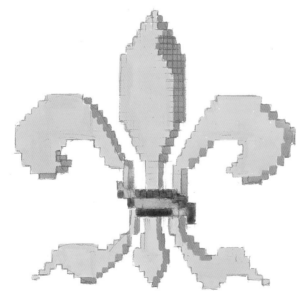

St Mark's, Swindon

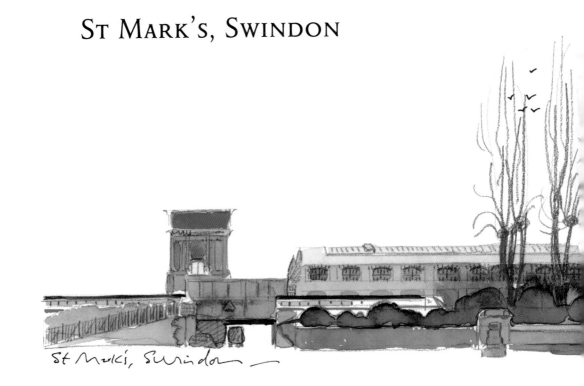

St Marks, Swindon

THE TRAIN DRAWS INTO the outskirts of a big town. It is Swindon. One hundred and twenty-eight years ago, there was nothing here at all but a canal and a place where two newly built railways joined, the Cheltenham and Great West Union Railway (the Gloucestershire line) and the London to Bristol line, known as the Great Western.

On a hill above the meadow was the old market town of Swindon. Then New Swindon was built in the meadow by the Great Western. It was a convenient point between Bristol and London. It consisted of sheds and a few rows of model cottages with open fields round them. These cottages are of Bath stone taken from the excavations of Box Tunnel. They still exist and are called the Company's Houses. They must form one of the earliest planned industrial estates in Britain.

The parishioners of St Philip and St Jacob in Bristol entreated the Great Western to build a church for their workers; directors found the money, subscriptions were raised, land was presented and by 1845, St Mark's Church was built.

There it stands today close beside the line, a stone building, all spikes and prickles outside, designed by Gilbert Scott who was then a young man and who lived to build hundreds of rather dull copy-book

100

churches all over Great Britain, and to build St Pancras Hotel, the Foreign Office in London and to 'restore' many cathedrals.

One cannot call it a convenient site. Whistles and passing trains disturb the services, diesel fumes blacken the leaves and tombstones and eat into the carved stonework of the steeple. No matter, it is a great church and though it isn't much to look at, it is for me the greatest church in England. For not carved stones nor screens and beautiful altars, nor lofty arcades, nor gilded canopies, but the priests who minister and the people who worship make a church great.

If ever I feel England is pagan, if ever I feel the poor old C. of E. is tottering to its grave, I revisit St Mark's, Swindon. That corrects the impression at once. A simple and definite faith is taught; St Mark's and its daughter churches are crowded. Swindon, so ugly to look at, to the eyes of the architectural student, glows golden as the New Jerusalem to the eyes that look beyond the brick and stone.

Swindon is largely a Christian town and much of the credit for that goes to the priests and people of St Mark's. It is not Sabbatarian and smug. It has its cinemas and theatres and art gallery and library and sports grounds and good old Swindon Town Football Club – but its churches are part of its life. That is the unusual thing about Swindon.

In the centenary book of St Mark's, there is a photograph of Canon Ponsonby wearing side whiskers and a beard that ran down his chin but not over it. This saintly Victorian priest (who died in 1945 aged nearly 100) caused St Mark's parish so to grow in faith that it built five other churches in New Swindon.

Two of them, St Paul's and St Augustine's, became separate parishes. He also caused the Wantage Sisters to open a mission house in Swindon.

The beautiful daughter church of St Mark's, St Luke's, was designed by W. A. Masters. Except for the railway works, St Luke's is the only fine interior, architecturally, in Swindon.

It is not about lovely St Luke's, nor about little St John's, I want to end this article. Up a steep hill going out of the New Town there is a church built of wood and called St Saviour's. That was erected in 1889–90, in six months, by St Mark's men, mostly railway workers.

When you consider that they did this in their spare time and for nothing, that some sacrificed their holidays and their working hours were from 6 am to 5.30 pm, you can imagine the faith that inspired them.

With foundations of faith like this, St Saviour's grew and in 1904 it had to be enlarged. Over one hundred once again set to work and the church was extended entirely by voluntary labour and in spare time.

I don't know why it is St Mark's parish hangs together and is a living community, full of life and spirit. Perhaps it is because Swindon is the right size for an industrial town, neither too big nor too small. Perhaps it is because the sort of work men do in a railways works – 'inside' as they called it in Swindon – perhaps it is because the men 'inside' do not do soul-destroying work such as one sees in motor factories where the ghastly chain-belt system persists. Whatever it is, I know that the people of Swindon first taught me not to be so la-de-da and architectural, not to judge people by the houses they live in, nor churches only by their architecture.

I would sooner be on my knees within the wooden walls of St Saviour's than leaning elegantly forward in a cushioned pew in an Oxford college chapel – that is to say if I am to realise there is something beyond this world worth thinking about.

On Hearing the Full Peal of Ten Bells from Christ Church, Swindon, Wilts.

Your peal of ten ring over then this town,
Ring on my men nor ever ring them down.
This winter chill, let sunset spill cold fire
On villa'd hill and on Sir Gilbert's spire,
So new, so high, so pure, so broach'd, so tall.
Long run the thunder of the bells through all!

Oh still white headstones on these fields of sound
Hear you the wedding joybells wheeling round?
Oh brick-built breeding boxes of new souls,
Hear how the pealing through the louvres rolls!
Now birth and death-reminding bells ring clear,
Loud under 'planes and over changing gear.

The City Churches

REN REBUILT FIFTY CHURCHES after the fire. Before the Germans came we had ourselves destroyed nineteen of these. The Germans completely gutted seventeen more.

Of those which survive for seeing today, I commend St Benet, Paul's Wharf, which is Welsh and inclined to be locked, St Mary-at-Hill, St Magnus the Martyr, St Margaret, Lothbury, St Margaret Pattens, St Peter, Cornhill, and St Stephen's, Walbrook, as being the most characteristic Wren churches, comparatively unmolested by Victorian 'restoration'. St Mary-at-Hill, which is nothing to look at outside and used to be surrounded by a smell of fish at Billingsgate, has the most untouched interior of all. Here the box pews, ironwork sword-rests, great west gallery, with its rich organ case, the fine pulpit and sounding board, the carved altar and altar-piece, recall Georgian London when beadles would hit the charity children sitting in the gallery with their staves, when merchants lived over their shops and offices and pageboys carried the prayer books of rich widows before them as they walked to worship.

There were more such unrestored churches in the City when I first knew it, for as a young boy I delighted to visit City churches, especially on a Sunday evening when single bells beat from moonlit steeples down gas-lit alleys, and choirboys would rush round corners through vestry archways. I can remember the row of fish-tail gas lights all along the triforium of St Bartholomew the Great; St Magnus the Martyr, when it had box pews and seemed very dead; and St Alban, Wood Street, with its green gas mantles and sparse congregation. In those days too, aged City men would come down from their brick, Italianate houses in Highbury or Streatham to worship in the City church where their fathers had worshipped before them. It was always my hope on some dark night to find a church which had escaped all the guide books and was there still in its classic splendour, with candles reflected in polished oak and cedar, with a parson in a black gown and bands, a beadle and the court of a City Company, robed and carrying a mace and swords. Once I thought I really had found the destroyed Wren church of St Matthew, Friday Street. Where is the oratory of Prebendary Hine-Haycock, preaching to the ranks of Blue Coat boys, tier upon tier in the galleries of Christ Church,

St Mary Abchurch, Cannon Street, LONDON

Newgate Street? Where is the dome of St Mildred, Bread Street, under which I sat in a high pew to hear the words of the Reverend Mr Richardson-Eyre, who would come in from some comfortable suburb to preach at Evensong on Sunday evening? Where is St Stephen, Coleman Street, the plainest and most despised of Wren's churches? Where the Evangelical raptures I enjoyed in St Bride's? Gone, gone, dead and bombed, only their peaceful memory now part of the history of our beautiful City. Yet the bombing has done one service to Wren which makes up for the destruction which tall buildings and the commercial policy of the Church have done to his forest of steeples gathered round St Paul's. If you stand at the corner of Wood Street near the back of Goldsmiths Hall, in the morning light or at night when the moon is up and there is a faint red glow in the sky from the West End, you will see what must be one of the most beautiful architectural sights in England. In the foreground withered willow-herb almost buries a pile of huge pink stones. Beyond this is Wren's exquisite stone steeple of St Vedast, Foster Lane, less elaborate but more satisfying than his famous steeple of St Mary-le-Bow, which stands quite near. Beyond St Vedast you will see the mighty dome of St Paul's and to the right the delicate and complicated silhouette of the north-west bell tower. And as you walk down Wood Street to Cheapside, St Vedast's steeple will glide past them and the hollows in it will open to show the sky beyond. Here architecture does what all the best architecture should do. It moves as you go past it and changes to make another and another and another perfect picture.

I have left to the last those City churches built since the time of Wren and which architecturally are some of the best and, though I dare to say it, more impressive and inventive as interiors than those by Wren himself. I think the first indignation at vandalism I ever felt was over the destruction of the eighteenth-century brick church of St Catherine Coleman, Fenchurch Street, which happened between the wars. In those days people could swallow Wren but nothing later. Georgian was thought little of and St Catherine's was a complete untouched Georgian interior, with all its old woodwork. Since then, thank goodness, our appreciation has widened. But the Church has destroyed eight of the seventeen post-Wren churches in the City of London. Mercifully the Germans did little damage to three of the best, St Mary Woolnoth, All Hallows, London Wall, and St Botolph, Aldersgate. Hawksmoor's church of St Mary Woolnoth by the Bank, with its twin square towers, is surely one of the most brilliant solutions to an awkwardly shaped site one could hope to see. The windowless side walls are full of interest. The interior, with its top lights, though it

St Laurence Jewry
Gresham Street

is in fact small, seems majestic and enormous. What is it that makes the City so different from all the rest of London? Mostly I think the City is different because of its churches, and these are used today more than ever, not just for concerts but as places in which to pray. If you go into a City church you will generally find someone on his knees.

St Mary at Hill, Eastcheap

St Bartholomew le Great, Smithfield

St Bartholomew's Hospital

The ghost of Rahere still walks in Bart's;
It gives an impulse to generous hearts,
It looks on pain with a pitying eye,
It teaches us never to fear to die.

Eight hundred years of compassion and care
Have hallowed its fountain, stones and Square.
Pray for us all as we near the gate –
St Bart the Less and St Bart the Great.

Old St Pancras church, London NW1

OLD ST PANCRAS CHURCH

OLD ST PANCRAS CHURCH, where Marie Taglioni was married to Comte Gilbert de Voisins on 14 July 1832, and where Joseph Grimaldi the dancing clown was wed, is hooted at by railways, swished past by trolley-buses, shaken by lorries, deafened by drays, smoked out by gas works, and now, at the time of writing, frowned upon by two cliffs of neo-modern borough council flats which are nearly complete. The Midland rolls into its Gothic terminus to the east, beyond that the Great Northern gets up steam for Cleethorpes. Behind where you are sitting in the picture, the London & North Western is making itself felt. What you are looking at is a parish church in the Anglo-Norman style of 1840, encasing and over-whelming what was once an ancient, dim little Middlesex fane not unlike Perivale, Northolt or Ickenham.

In the churchyard outside, which is half sooty municipal garden and too cemeterial for a nice progressive reccy-ground, lies the great

late Georgian architect Sir John Soane. The tomb is of his own design, enormous and in his strange Soanean classic style, which has so much influenced modern Scandinavian architecture.

The church inside has been altered by bombing which smashed the Victorian stained glass windows. Now the glass is clear. Sooty thorns show through the east window. The interior walls have been whitened, the floors sensitively renewed with wood blocks and huge grave slabs of slate and stone. An altar stone, said to have been dedicated by St Augustine in 602, has been dug out of a wall of the church and replaced on the high altar. The Victorian iron screen has been gilded, and very nice it looks. There is decoration in the style of the late Martin Travers. The Blessed Sacrament is here, so it is an easy church for praying. It is a core of quiet in the noise of transport. The ironwork entrance gate is mostly eighteenth-century, removed I suppose, from some merchant's country house in the parish. And inside the church with the monuments of these seventeenth and eighteenth century citizens looking down from the white walls, it is easy to be back in the days when this was St Pancras-in-the-Fields and people came to be wedded or were carried to the font or a hole in the earth, from a newly built stucco box or older brown brick Middlesex farm.

Holy Trinity, Sloane Street, MCMVII

An Acolyte singeth
Light six white tapers with the Flame of Art,
Send incense wreathing to the lily flowers,
And, with your cool hands white,
Swing the warm censer round my bruised heart,
Drop, dove-grey eyes, your penitential showers
On this pale acolyte.

A confirmandus continueth
The tall red house soars upward to the stars,
The doors are chased with sardonyx and gold,
And in the long white room
Thin drapery draws backward to unfold
Cadogan Square between the window-bars
And Whistler's mother knitting in the gloom.

The Priest endeth
How many hearts turn Motherward to-day?
(Red roses faint not on your twining stems!)
Bronze triptych doors unswing!
Wait, restive heart, wait, rounded lips, to pray,
Mid beaten copper interest with gems
Behold! Behold! your King!

Holy Trinity, Sloane Street

Bishop, archdeacon, rector, wardens, mayor
Guardians of Chelsea's noblest house of prayer,

You who your church's vastness deplore
'Should we not sell and give it to the poor?'

Recall, despite your practical suggestion
Which the disciple was who asked that question.

St Barnabas Church

THE SLENDER CAMPANILE OF St Barnabas Church dominates Jericho and it is a nice experience on a Sunday morning to hear the tubular bells call over the housetops, to see the unperturbed Jericho-dwellers polishing up a knocker and the many students of liturgiology walking down Cardigan Street from the University. Not that St Barnabas does nothing for the parish: it has the most live and active social organization of all Oxford churches: but high mass at 11 on Sunday is an Oxford 'sight' and the University, on that day in the week, still comes to St Barnabas as it did, in greater numbers, when this was a pioneer church of the Catholic Revival.

The building is in the Lombardic style and must have looked better when its brick exterior was clean and it stood Guardi-like above the Oxford Canal (see photograph by entrance). It was opened in 1869. The architect was Sir A. Blomfield and I have no hesitation in saying St Barnabas is far the best of his work I have seen — and I have seen much.

St Barnabas Church, Oxford

How long was the peril, how breathless the day,
In topaz and beryl, the sun dies away,
His rays lying static at quarter to six
On polychromatical lacing of bricks.
Good Lord, as the angelus floats down the road
Byzantine St Barnabas, be Thine Abode.

Where once the fritillaries hung in the grass
A baldachin pillar is guarding the Mass.
Farewell to blue meadows we loved not enough,
And elms in whose shadows were Glanville and Clough
Not poets but clergymen hastened to meet
Thy redden'd remorselessness, Cardigan Street.

St Barnabas Church, OXFORD

St Mary the Virgin Church

THE BUILDING IS FREQUENTLY mistaken for the Cathedral. Its spire and many pinnacles are the most prominent feature of the High Street. The entrance porch was erected in 1637, the most baroque construction in Oxford. Archbishop Laud got into considerable trouble from Puritans for causing the statue of the Virgin and Holy Child to be placed in the niche. Notice the wrought iron gates.

The interior has lost its character since many of the excellent box-pews, designed by Thomas Plowman from 1826–1828, were removed in the recent 'restoration' by Sir Charles Nicholson. The stained glass is all too prominent and none too lovely. The west window by Kempe (1891) is to Dean Burgon, author of the well known line in a prize poem, 'A rose-red city half as old as time'.

The N.E. corner of this church is the heart of the University. Hence the organization spread out. In this corner was a two storey building. From the fourteenth to the seventeenth centuries it was the Convocation House. Upstairs was the University Library from the fourteenth to the fifteenth century, then it was the archive room till the seventeenth.

In Catholic days 'the various chapels of St. Mary's were assigned to the different Faculties for their deliberations, and the Congregation of all the Faculties, Regents (i.e., teachers) and non-Regents alike, met in the choir, forming the supreme governing body of the University'.

Since then it has been a powder magazine for the Civil War, a type-store, a book-seller's storeroom, a grammar school, a fire station, a law lecture room, a chapel, a parish room, a chapel.

Various awe-inspiring scenes have occurred here: Cranmer in 1555 was placed on a low platform opposite the pulpit to have a sermon preached against him after his trial; Queen Elizabeth made a speech in Latin after listening for three days to learned disputes here; Dr. Sacheverell preached here; Rev. John Wesley preached here; Rev. John Keble started the Oxford Movement here; Rev. John Henry Newman was vicar here and crowded the church out.

The University sermon is preached here on Sundays at 10.30 a.m. during Full Term and at the Assizes. The Proctors and Vice-Chancellor are obliged to attend. The preacher wears a black gown. A Latin Litany is said and a Latin sermon is preached once a year.

OxFORD: St Mary the Virgin from the Radcliffe Camera

Nonconformist Architecture

THE EARLIEST NONCONFORMIST PLACES of worship, built specifically for worship, are all later than 1650. They were designed as preaching houses. Usually they are plain, often delicate, compositions with windows on three sides and the pulpit approached by steps against the fourth. Sometimes there is a clear space in the middle of the room, for a communion table. Galleries round three sides were often added.

In their simplest form, in the Quaker meeting houses where the doctrine of the Society demanded no worldly ostentation whatever, the buildings have the quality of a well-scoured farmhouse kitchen – a stone or tiled floor, scrubbed oak open seats, white walls and clear glass windows. Sometimes in the older meeting houses the walls were covered to the height of a man's shoulder with rush matting. One might say the Quakers were the Cistercians of Nonconformist builders. The Unitarians (then Presbyterians) were the Cluniacs. They did not despise decorative treatment, or angels' heads as exterior keystones. The first Methodist preaching house was not built until 1739 in Bristol and it survives almost as it was. This building is the first of a larger series of chapels than that of the first group and I think we might name it the first building of the architecture of Enthusiasm.

When John Wesley died in 1791 there were 60,000 Methodists in Great Britain and 11,000 in Ireland; most of them were in the northern and western counties of England and in the north and east of Ireland. These people were mostly men who had not previously bothered about spiritual matters; they were workers from early and dismal, industrial districts, half starved people who saw no hope of ease and happiness in this life and were attracted by the promises of indescribable ease and happiness in the next. Where Wesley or Whitfield lifted their voices, people fell down with groans and wrestled with the Evil One.

The first chapels to be built by the Methodists were meant to serve as overflow preaching houses when the Established church was either too far distant, too hostile, or too small in seating capacity for the numbers attracted by the new preaching. Like the buildings of the earlier group, they were designed to seat as many people as possible within a good view of the pulpit. Crosses, altars and decoration were

friends' Meeting-House, JORDANS, Chalfont St Giles, Bucks

regarded as unnecessary, for there were such things at the Parish church. They were large, rather flimsy buildings, and did not scorn a bit of carpenter's or plasterer's moulding here and there by way of internal embellishment. They were erected mostly by pious merchants or landowners whose enthusiasm extended to their pockets.

When great cities prospered after the depression following the Napoleonic wars, and Methodist merchants grew richer, stately chapels were built in the chastest Greek or Commissioner's Perpendicular. Liverpool, Manchester, London and Bristol still contain a number.

Where, in the country and in small towns, there was less wealthy patronage for the enthusiastic chapels, the buildings were unpretentious 'barn-like' structures. The interiors were often wholly delightful: pale pink walls, Chippendale Gothic ceilings, high grained-oak pews, white gallery fronts and double rows of clear glass sash-windows round three sides of the building, and against the blank fourth wall a fine mahogany pulpit.

At last we come to the most interesting phase of Nonconformist architecture, that which shows more surely than any Victorian Established church, whether high, low, broad, Gothic, Romanesque or Classic, what was the true architecture of the people. Not since medieval days had the people clubbed together to adorn a place of worship and this time it was not a shrine but a preaching house. In mining districts and lonely villages of Wales, among the gleaming granite and slate of Cornwall, down the brick-red streets of Leeds, Belfast, Liverpool and Manchester, in almost every city and corrugated suburb of Great Britain and the Six Counties Area, wedged in on the common land beside country houses and red and blue among the thatched roofs of southern villages or the stone roofs of northern ones, stand the chapels of the mid-nineteenth century. Despised by architects, ignored by guide books, too briefly mentioned by directories, these variegated conventicles are witnesses of the taste of industrial Britain. They try to ape nothing. They were anxious not to look like the church, which held them in contempt; nor like a house, for they were places of worship; nor like a theatre, for they were sacred piles. They succeeded in looking like what they are – chapels, so that the most unobservant traveller can tell a chapel from any other building in the street.

The nineteenth century was a period of great religious revivals and this is not the place to examine their causes. The chapels were built as the result of those revivals and they represent pennies saved which might otherwise have been spent on drink, or profits from tiny shops and lean farms and gardens where farm workers had toiled until sun-down. All sorts of people connected with the chapel contributed their bit; the local builder supplied the labour and the plan; the ironmonger the cast iron railings and the lamps; the timber merchant the wood; a builders' merchant gave of his best in ridge tiles, stonecaps and dress-ings; another builder undertook to look out coloured glass and win-dow frames; carpenters in the congregation fixed the pews; painters did the graining and the stencilling; the linen draper looked to the cushions and coverings; and when it was all finished the stationer at his own steam press produced the illustrated account of the opening ceremony. Those who had no trade or craft directly connected with the chapel subscribed all they could. Pitchpine pews, green walls, brass, Lombardic and handsomely-painted pulpit, lamp brackets, car-peted alleys, stencilled texts and homeliness – it was better than the

Wesley's New Room, 1739-48, Bristol

best house in the circuit. And yet it was built more on the lines of a pre-Reformation Catholic church than the correctest Pugin or boldest Butterfield. These were indeed the thresholds of a better world than this, the brick and stone expression of individual conversion and acceptance, not the stilted copying of a religion based on Prayer Books and Missals and idol worship. This was the Liberal vote.

It would be a pleasure to try to trace some individuality of style belonging to each of the denominations of Nonconformity. But this is possible only in the most general way. In England the five chief divisions are Methodist, Congregational, Baptist, Brethren and other denominations.

The Methodist church today is a Union of various Methodist Societies which sprang up so soon as Wesley's followers started to ordain their own ministers without the medium of a Bishop of the Church of England. The oldest were the Wesleyan Methodists and on the whole they were the richest. Their buildings, when they are not of the chaste, enthusiastic period, were rebuilt quite late in the nineteenth century and in a solid style generally faintly echoing the ancient Gothic style of the Established Church, externally at any rate.

The Primitive Methodists broke from the Wesleyans in 1810. They were humbler and more wildly enthusiastic people than the Wesleyans. They favoured camp meetings, female preachers, and the uttering of loud ejaculations during inspired prayers. By 1851 they had 3,000 chapels. Their architecture is very rarely Gothic; they are often tiny structures on waste spaces by the roadside in the country or high flimsy-looking Italianate barns in the towns. They employed architects more rarely than any other denomination.

The United Methodists arose in 1850 and were an amalgamation of various offshoots from the original society. Their buildings were humbler than those of the Wesleyans and abound in Cornwall and Durham.

Humbler too, but unclassifiable, are the buildings of the various other branches of Methodism, now united, except for Calvinistic, in the Methodist Church. That at Frome is famous. Until about 1860 most Congregational churches were built in a classic style, a public-worship variation of the middle class villa of the date, running through from Greek to Roman and Italianate. Possibly because there was something traditional and respectable about Gothic towards the latter half of the last century, later Congregational churches are Gothic, and Basil Champneys' Mansfield College, Oxford (1889–90) is one of the best bits of Perpendicular Revival in that city.

The Baptists roused themselves in the late eighteenth century when

Cote Baptist Church, Oxon

they started their great missionary effort. The General Baptists (not to be confused with the Strict and Particular Baptists, who are small and Calvinistic) are the largest body of Nonconformists in the world. Their new churches had some of the traditionalism of the Congregationals. They usually built large classic conventicles of which that at Newington Butts was, as it were, the cathedral.

125

BE thou give thee
faithful a Crown
unto of life
death REV
and I will II. c 10.

Welsh Congregational Chapel, Maesyronen nr Clyro

Plymouth Brethren are one of the few Nonconformist bodies still increasing. They are divided among themselves, but their meeting places can be distinguished from others by the board which generally says:

THE LORD'S DAY.

Breaking of Bread, 11 a.m

The Gospel will be preached here (God Willing) 6.30 p.m.

The sect is of nineteenth-century origin and its buildings are a cross between the Quaker meeting house and the Primitive Methodist chapel.

In Wales the chapel architecture of the nineteenth century is not denominational but racial. It is hardly ever architect-designed, but the product of a local contractor who has made the fullest use of an illustrated catalogue. The congregations are often, to this day, in debt to the contractor for his work. The buildings are essentially local and vary with the districts. They have the quality of good sign-writing and a vigorous style of their own. In one the designer will have concentrated on emphasising the windows, in another on bringing out the texture of the stone, in another on arranging ingeniously the doors and windows of the west front, in another on colouring the outside plaster. These buildings have beauty which is apart from date and akin to the naïveté of the Douanier Rousseau.

Since about 1910 there has been a liturgical movement in many Nonconformist churches and this has affected new building. Unitarian churches now have chancels; Holy Tables have bunches of flowers on them and the pulpit is losing its old position of predominance. Even Methodist churches have a sober look and may be mistaken, externally, for a mission church of the Church of England. The two styles usually adopted are either Perpendicular with a touch of *art nouveau* and terra-cotta about it, or Christian Science Romanesque. Indeed the new buildings of Nonconformity lack the individuality and strong character of those scrubbed conventicles of the seventeenth and eighteenth centuries or the gigantic preaching houses of the Victorian age.

Countess of Huntingdon Chapel / WORCESTER

Calvinistic Evensong

The six bells stopped, and in the dark I heard
Cold silence wait the Calvinistic word;
For Calvin now the soft oil lamps are lit
Hands on their hymnals six old women sit.
Black gowned and sinister, he now appears
Curate-in-charge of aged parish fears.
Let, unaccompanied, that psalm begin
Which deals most harshly with the fruits of sin!
Boy! pump the organ! let the anthem flow
With promise for the chosen saints below!
Pregnant with warning the globed elm trees wait
Fresh coffin-wood beside the churchyard gate.
And that mauve hat three cherries decorate
Next week shall topple from its trembling perch
While wet fields reek like some long empty church.

Our Padre

Our padre is an old sky pilot,
    Severely now they've clipped his wings,
But still the flagstaff in the Rect'ry garden
    Points to Higher Things.

Still he has got a hearty handshake;
    Still he wears his medals and a stole;
His voice would reach to Heaven, *and* make
    The Rock of Ages Roll.

He's too sincere to join the high church
    Worshipping idols for the Lord,
And, though the lowest church is my church,
    Our padre's Broad.

Our padre is an old sky pilot,
    He's tied a reef knot round my heart,
We'll be rocked up to Heaven on a rare old tune –
    Come on – take part!

CHORUS (*Sung*) Pull for the shore, sailor, pull for the shore!
    Heed not the raging billow, bend to the oar!
Bend to the oar before the padre!
    Proud, with the padre rowing stroke!
Good old padre! God for the services!
    Row like smoke!

Blame the Vicar

When things go wrong it's rather tame
To find we are ourselves to blame,
It gets the trouble over quicker
To go and blame things on the Vicar.
The Vicar, after all, is paid
To keep us bright and undismayed.
The Vicar is more virtuous too
Than lay folks such as me and you.
He never swears, he never drinks,
He never *should* say what he thinks.
His collar is the wrong way round,
And that is why he's simply bound
To be the sort of person who
Has nothing very much to do
But take the blame for what goes wrong
And sing in tune at Evensong.

For what's a Vicar really for
Except to cheer us up? What's more,
He shouldn't ever, ever tell
If there is such a place as Hell,
For if there is it's certain he
Will go to it as well as we.
The Vicar should be all pretence
And never, never give offence.
To preach on Sunday is his task
And lend his mower when we ask
And organize our village fêtes
And sing at Christmas with the waits
And in his car to give us lifts
And when we quarrel, heal the rifts.
To keep his family alive
He should industriously strive
In that enormous house he gets,
And he should always pay his debts,
For he has quite six pounds a week,
And when we're rude he should be meek
And always turn the other cheek.
He should be neat and nicely dressed
With polished shoes and trousers pressed,
For we look up to him as higher
Than anyone, except the Squire.
    Dear People, who have read so far,
I know how really kind you are,
I hope that you are always seeing
Your Vicar as a human being,
Making allowances when he
Does things with which you don't agree.
But there are lots of people who

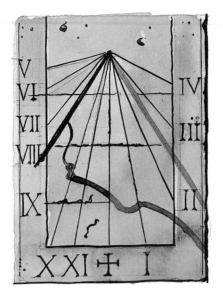

Are not so kind to him as you.
So in conclusion you shall hear
About a parish somewhat near,
Perhaps your own or maybe not,
And of the Vicars that it got.

   One parson came and people said,
'Alas! Our former Vicar's dead!
And this new man is far more "Low"
Than dear old Reverend so-and-so,
And far too earnest in his preaching,
We do not really like his teaching,
He seems to think we're simply fools
Who've never been to Sunday Schools.'
That Vicar left, and by and by
A new one came, 'He's much too "High",'
The people said, 'too like a saint,
His incense makes our Mavis faint.'

So now he's left and they're alone
Without a Vicar of their own.
The living's been amalgamated
With one next door they've always hated.

Notes and Acknowledgements

This book includes only an edited selection of John Betjeman's writings on the Church. The prose passages are in many cases abridged sections from longer works. Where essential they have been lightly edited to retain the original sense in their shortened form. For Betjeman the Church was a subject of inexhaustible fascination in all its aspects – the churches themselves, church history, beliefs, ritual, and people both clergy and lay. The reader can readily find more on the Church in other books by him, especially *Collected Poems, Church Poems*, and the *Guide to English Parish Churches*.

The contents of this book are taken from the following: 'Church Crawling' (originally part of 'The Church of St Protus and St Hyacinth, at Blisland, Cornwall'), 'The Church of St John the Baptist at Mildenhall, Wiltshire', 'The Church of St Protus etc.', 'In Praise of the Victorians' and 'St Mark's, Swindon' are from *West Country Churches* (published also in slightly different form in *First and Last Loves*). 'The Old Churches', 'The Churchyard', 'The Outside of the Church', 'The Bells' 'The Interior Today', 'The Interior in 1860', 'The Church in Georgian Times', 'The Church in the Fifteenth Century', 'The Church before the Fifteenth Century', and 'The Newer Churches' are from the Introduction to the *Guide to English Parish Churches* and are printed here by permission of HarperCollins. 'Bristol', 'Uffington', 'On Leaving Wantage', 'Hymn', 'Verses Turned in Aid of a Public Subscription towards the Restoration of the Church of St Katherine, Chiselhampton, Oxon.', 'Diary of a Church Mouse','Christmas','St Saviour's, Aberdeen Park, Highbury, London N.', 'Undenominational', 'Sunday Afternoon in St Enodoc Church, Cornwall', 'On Hearing the Full Peal of Ten Bells from Christ Church, Swindon, Wilts.', 'Holy Trinity, Sloane Street, MCMVII', 'St Barnabas Church, Oxford', 'Calvinistic Evensong', and 'Our Padre' are from *Collected Poems*. 'Churchyards', 'Septuagesima', 'St Bartholomew's Hospital', and 'Blame the Vicar' are from *Church Poems*. 'St Endellion' and 'Nonconformist Architecture' are from *First and Last Loves*. 'The City Churches', 'Old St Pancras Church' and 'Holy Trinity, Sloane Street' are from *Betjeman's London*, and 'St Barnabas Church' and 'St Mary the Virgin Church' are from *An Oxford University Chest*, printed here by permission of the Oxford University Press.

Naturally, not all the churches described are as they were when Betjeman wrote about them. For instance, St Saviour's Aberdeen Park is now artists' studios owned by the Florence Trust, a charity providing workspace for young, usually struggling artists. St Saviour's, described in 'St Mark's, Swindon', has been replaced by a DIY-type edifice built perhaps in the 1960s. There have been no services in the Countess of Huntingdon Chapel since 1976. In poor repair, it was restored as a concert hall. Its 'unique and irreplaceable' Nicholson organ has been restored as well.

ILLUSTRATIONS

(The following illustrations are those without captions in the text)